IELTS Academic Writing Book with IELTS Grammar Preparation & Sample Essays

Best IELTS Essay Writing Practice Book for a Band 9 Score on Task 1 and Task 2

IELTS is jointly owned by the British Council, IDP: IELTS Australia, and Cambridge English Language Assessments, which are neither affiliated with nor endorse this publication.

IELTS Academic Writing Book with IELTS Grammar Preparation & Sample Essays: Best IELTS Essay Writing Practice Book for a Band 9 Score on Task 1 and Task 2

© COPYRIGHT 1995, 2014, 2021. IELTS Success Associates dba www.examsam.com

All rights reserved. No part of this publication may be reproduced, stored in a retrieval system or transmitted, in any form or by any means, electronic, mechanical, photocopying, recording or otherwise.

ISBN: 978-1-949282-77-1

COPYRIGHT NOTICE TO EDUCATORS: Please respect copyright law. Under no circumstances may you make copies of these materials for distribution to or use by students. Should you wish to use the materials with students, you are required to purchase a copy of this publication for each of your students.

NOTE: IELTS is jointly owned by the British Council, IDP: IELTS Australia, and Cambridge English Language Assessments, which are neither affiliated with nor endorse this publication.

TABLE OF CONTENTS

PART 1 – WRITING THE IELTS ESSAYS:

IELTS Essay Format & Question Types	1
How Your IELTS Essays Are Scored	4
How to Avoid Common Essay Errors and Raise Your Score	6

PART 2 – GRAMMAR PREPARATION:

Grammar on the IELTS Writing Test	9
Avoiding Misplaced Modifiers	9
Pronoun-Antecedent Agreement	10
Pronoun Usage – Correct Use of *Its* and *It's*	10
Pronoun Usage – Correct Use of *Their*, *There* and *They're*	11
Pronoun Usage – Avoiding "You" and "Your"	12
Pronoun Usage – Demonstrative Pronouns	12
Pronoun Usage – Relative Pronouns	13
Punctuation – Avoiding the Parenthetical	14
Punctuation – Using the Apostrophe for Possessive Forms	15
Punctuation – Using Colons and Semicolons	16
Punctuation – Using Commas with Dates and Locations	16
Punctuation – Using Commas for Items in a Series	16
Punctuation and Independent Clauses	17
Restrictive and Non-restrictive Modifiers	18

Sentence Fragments	18
Subject-Verb Agreement	19
Grammar and Punctuation Exercises	21
Grammar and Punctuation Exercises - Answers	23

PART 3 – IELTS LANGUAGE PRACTICE:

How to Use Phrases, Clauses and Cohesive Devices to Develop Your Sentences	25
Sentence Linkers	25
Phrase Linkers	26
Subordinators	28
Cohesive Devices by Category	29
Sentence Development Exercises	35
Sentence Development Exercises – Answers & Explanations	40

PART 4 – TASK 1 ESSAYS:

The Different Types of Data Representation	49
Analysing the Data Before You Write	49
How to Structure the Task 1 Essay	50
How to Introduce the Data	51
How to Select and Comment on Significant Details	53
How to Describe Overall Trends	55
Task 1 – Sample Response	56

Useful Words and Phrases for Writing Task 1   57

PART 5 – TASK 2 ESSAYS:

Task 2 Essay Structure   59

Creating Effective Thesis Statements   61

Thesis Statement – Exercises and Answers   63

Writing the Introduction   65

Writing the Introduction – Exercises and Answers   66

Organising the Main Body   69

Elaboration in the Body Paragraphs   70

Elaboration of Supporting Points – Exercises and Answers   72

Writing the Main Body Paragraphs – Exercises and Answers   75

Writing Clear and Concise Topic Sentences   80

Topic Sentences – Exercises and Answers   83

Writing the Conclusion   86

Writing the Conclusion – Exercises and Answers   87

Task 2 – Sample Essay   91

PART 6 – IELTS WRITING PRACTICE TESTS:

IELTS Writing Practice Test 1 – Task 1   94

IELTS Writing Practice Test 1 – Task 2   95

Model Essays for Writing Practice Test 1   96

Comments on the Model Practice Test 1 Essays   99

IELTS Writing Practice Test 2 – Task 1	100
IELTS Writing Practice Test 2 – Task 2	101
Model Essays for Writing Practice Test 2	102
Comments on the Model Practice Test 2 Essays	105
IELTS Writing Practice Test 3 – Task 1	106
IELTS Writing Practice Test 3 – Task 2	107
Model Essays for Writing Practice Test 3	108
Comments on the Model Practice Test 3 Essays	111

PART 7 – REVIEW OF VERB USAGE AND TENSE:

Verb tense and usage – Active voice:

Present simple tense	112
Past simple tense	112
Future simple tense	113
Present perfect tense	114
Past perfect tense	114
Future perfect tense	116
Present simple progressive	117
Past simple progressive	117
Future simple progressive	118
Present perfect progressive	119

Verb tense and usage – Passive voice:

    Present simple passive — 120

    Past simple passive — 120

    Future simple passive — 121

    Future passive with is/are — 121

    Present simple progressive passive — 121

    Past simple progressive passive — 121

    Present perfect passive — 122

    Past perfect passive — 122

Gerunds and Infinitives — 123

Modal verbs — 129

Phrasal verbs and prepositions — 133

PART 8 – ADDITIONAL GRAMMAR EXERCISES:

    Gerunds and Infinitives – Exercises — 134

    Modal Verbs – Exercises — 136

    Past Perfect – Exercises — 138

    Phrasal Verbs – Exercises — 140

    Prepositions – Exercises — 146

    Third Conditional – Exercises — 149

    Answers to the Grammar Exercises — 151

BONUS MATERIAL: Essay Correction Exercises — 158

Answers to the Essay Correction Exercises — 190

PART 1 – WRITING THE IELTS ESSAYS

IELTS Essay Format & Question Types

IELTS essay writing

Your IELTS test will include a written essay component that consists of two tasks.

Task 1 of the IELTS Academic Module is a data analysis essay.

Task 2 of both the IELTS Academic and General Training Modules is a persuasive or argumentative essay.

The purpose of the essays is to assess your ability to express your thoughts in a reasoned and academic manner.

The IELTS assesses this skill because academic writing is essential for success at British universities.

If you perform poorly on your IELTS essay, you may need to take developmental English classes during your first year of studies.

You can spend a great deal of time attending these classes. In addition, the developmental classes are usually non-credit, so they won't count towards your degree.

Test administration

You will write your essay on paper. Study aids, such as dictionaries or grammar books, are not permitted.

Time limit

You will be given 60 minutes to plan, write and edit both of your essays. You should devote 20 minutes to writing task 1 and 40 minutes to writing task 2.

Word count

Your task 1 essay should normally be at least 150 words, while your task 2 essay should be a minimum of 250 words long.

Essay task 1

For the first essay, you will see a graph or other visual data and will need to write about the information, using your own words.

Essay task 2

The essay question 2 will usually ask you to take a position on a familiar topic, such as problems commonly faced by students or dilemmas encountered by the individual in society.

You will need to take a stand on the issue presented and support your viewpoint with reasons and examples.

Sample essay questions are provided on the following page.

Here is a sample task 1 IELTS Academic essay question:

Instructions: The table below shows the number of union members per year for Oxfordshire, Wiltshire, Somerset and the Remaining Counties in England from 1994 to 2014. Please analyse the data and comment on its significant characteristics.

Union Members in Oxfordshire, Wiltshire, Somerset and Remaining Counties				
Year	Oxfordshire	Wiltshire	Somerset	Remaining Counties
1994	2,365	1,981	3,687	52,187
1999	1,987	1,945	3,522	48,233
2004	1,784	1,915	3,623	51,505
2009	1,801	1,899	3,547	50,689
2014	1,121	1,892	3,601	49,117

Here is a sample task 2 IELTS essay question:

Most people have access to computers and mobile phones on a daily basis, making email and text messaging extremely popular. While some argue that email and texting are now the most convenient forms of personal communication, others believe that electronic communication technology is often used inappropriately. Write an essay for an audience of educated adults in which you take a position on this topic. Be sure to provide reasons and examples to support your viewpoint.

We will see sample responses to these essay topics in the subsequent sections of this publication.

How Your IELTS Essays Are Scored

Your essay will be scored by an experienced IELTS examiner.

The following characteristics of your essay will be assessed:

1. Task completion – This means that your essay should answer the question that has been posed. You will need to express your main idea in a clear way in the introduction of the essay.

   For your task 2 essay, the examiner will look for a thesis statement in the first paragraph of your essay. You also need to be sure that you take stand on one side of the issue or the other. Your score will not be affected by the position you take.

   It is extremely important to elaborate on the main idea of your essay and maintain your point of view throughout your writing. Your essay should include examples and explanations that illustrate and support your viewpoint.

2. Rhetorical coherence and cohesion – Your essay should be divided into paragraphs, which have been set out in an organised manner. Each body paragraph should contain a point that supports your main idea. You should also include a conclusion that sums up the essay.

3. <u>Sentence construction and grammar</u> – You should write long and developed sentences that demonstrate a variety of sentence patterns. You should avoid repeatedly beginning your sentences in the same way, such as "I think that".

   The examiner will look to see whether you have used a variety of sentence patterns.

   Your essay should be grammatically accurate and punctuated correctly. Your spelling should also be correct.

4. <u>Lexical level</u> – Your essay needs to address the concerns of your target audience. You need to be sure that you have used high-level academic vocabulary in order to achieve this purpose.

How to Avoid Common Essay Errors and Raise Your Score

In the previous section, we talked about the characteristics of a well-written IELTS essay.

However, you may also wonder which aspects of an essay would be scored poorly by the examiners.

These errors most commonly cause students to receive a low score on the IELTS task 2 essay:

1. The essay fails to express a clear point of view or provides a viewpoint that cannot be logically supported.

   Tip: You can avoid this error by giving a clear thesis statement in the first paragraph of your essay.

2. The essay is written in a tone and style that is not suitable for an academic audience.

   Tip: Achieving the correct tone and style means that you need to avoid using informal or conversational expressions in your writing. Examples of informal language include words like "brilliant" or "mate".

3. The reasons or examples provided in the essay are flawed because they do not support the student's main point.

Tip: Be sure that your reasons and examples are closely related to your main idea and to the essay topic. For instance, if you are asked whether art programs should be supported in schools, and then go on to talk about physical education programs because you believe they are similar to art programs, your reasoning would be flawed.

4. The essay is disorganised and therefore difficult to read and score.

   Tip: You can avoid this error by brainstorming your ideas and planning your essay before you begin writing.

5. The essay contains errors in sentence construction or contains only simple or repetitive sentence structures.

   Tip: Try to avoid writing every sentence of your essay in the subject-verb-object sentence pattern. In order to avoid this shortcoming, you can begin sentences with words and phrases like "although" or "because of this".

6. The essay does not demonstrate a complex thought process.

   Tip: Be sure that you give persuasive reasons and examples to express and support your position.

7. The essay contains errors in spelling, grammar and punctuation.

Tip: If you have weaknesses in these areas, you should spend more time studying the "Grammar Preparation" and "IELTS Language Practice" sections of this study guide.

PART 2 – GRAMMAR PREPARATION

Using Correct Grammar and Punctuation

Part 2 reviews some of the basic rules of grammar, punctuation and sentence construction that are assessed in your IELTS essays.

To review verb tense and usage, please refer to Part 7 of this publication.

There are exercises at the end of Part 2, and additional exercises on advanced grammar are provided in Part 8 of this book.

Avoiding Misplaced Modifiers

> Modifiers are descriptive phrases. The modifier should always be placed directly before or after the noun to which it relates.

Now look at the examples.

CORRECT: Like most of western Scotland, the Hebrides are not very densely populated.

INCORRECT: Like most of western Scotland, there isn't a large population in the Hebrides.

The phrase "like most of western Scotland" is an adjectival phrase that modifies the noun phrase "the Hebrides".

Therefore, "the Hebrides" must come directly after the comma.

Here are two more examples:

CORRECT: While waiting at the bus stop, a senior citizen was mugged.

INCORRECT: While waiting at the bus stop, a mugging took place.

The adverbial phrase "while waiting at the bus stop" modifies the noun phrase "a senior citizen", so this noun phrase needs to come after the adverbial phrase.

Pronoun-Antecedent Agreement

> Pronouns are words like the following: he, she, it, they and them.
> An antecedent is a phrase that precedes the pronoun in the sentence.

Pronouns must agree with their antecedents.

Now look at the examples below.

CORRECT: Each student needs to bring his or her identification to the placement test.

INCORRECT: Each student needs to bring their identification to the placement test.

The antecedent "each student" is singular, so the singular pronouns "his" or "her" should follow this antecedent.

Pronoun Usage – Correct Use of *Its* and *It's*

> "Its" is a possessive pronoun, while "it's" is a contraction of "it is".

CORRECT: It's high time you started to study.

INCORRECT: Its high time you started to study.

The sentence could also be stated as follows: It is high time you started to study.

Since the contracted form of "it is" can be used in the alternative sentence above, "it's" is the correct form.

CORRECT: A snake sheds its skin at least once a year.

INCORRECT: A snake sheds it's skin at least once a year.

"Its" is a possessive pronoun referring to the snake, so the apostrophe should not be used.

Pronoun Usage – Correct Use of *Their*, *There* and *They're*

> "Their" is a plural possessive pronoun. "There" is used to describe the location of something. "They're" is a contraction of "they are".

CORRECT: Their house is made of brick and concrete.

INCORRECT: There house is made of brick and concrete.

INCORRECT: They're house is made of brick and concrete.

In this case, "their" is the possessive pronoun explaining to whom the house belongs.

CORRECT: He attended university with his cousins living there in Birmingham.

INCORRECT: He attended university with his cousins living their in Birmingham.

INCORRECT: He attended university with his cousins living they're in Birmingham.

"There" is referring to the city of Birmingham in the example above, so it is used to talk about the location.

CORRECT: They're away on holiday at the moment.

INCORRECT: Their away on holiday at the moment.

INCORRECT: There away on holiday at the moment.

The sentence could also be written as follows: They are away on holiday at the moment.

"They're" is a contraction of "they are", so the apostrophe needs to be used.

Pronoun Usage – Avoiding "You" and "Your"

> The pronouns "you" and "your" are informal and should generally be avoided in academic writing when referring to a person in general.

FORMAL: Students should plan in advance if they intend to do well on the project.

INFORMAL: You should plan in advance if you intend to do well on the project.

Pronoun Usage – Demonstrative Pronouns

> Demonstrative pronouns include the following words: this, that, these, those

"This" is used for a singular item that is nearby. "That" is used for singular items that are further away in time or space.

SINGULAR: This book that I have here is really interesting.

PLURAL: That book on the table over there is really interesting.

"These" is used for plural items that are nearby. "Those" is used for plural items that are further away in time or space.

SINGULAR: These pictures in my purse were taken on our holiday.

PLURAL: Those pictures on the wall were taken on our holiday.

Avoid using "them" instead of "those":

INCORRECT: Them pictures on the wall were taken on our holiday.

Pronoun Usage – Relative Pronouns

Relative pronouns include the following: which, that, who, whom, whose

> "Which" and "that" are used to describe things, and "who" and "whom" are used to describe people. "Whose" is used for people or things.

WHICH: Last night, I watched a romantic-comedy movie which was really funny.

THAT: Last night, I watched a romantic-comedy movie that was really funny.

WHO: Susan always remains calm under pressure, unlike Tom, who is always so nervous.

"Who" is used because we are describing the person. This is known as the nominative case.

WHOM: To whom should the report be given?

"Whom" is used because the person is receiving an action, which in this case is receiving the report. This is known as the accusative case.

WHOSE: I went out for lunch with Marta, whose parents are from Costa Rica.

WHOSE: I went out for lunch yesterday at that new restaurant, whose name I don't remember.

Please be sure to look at the section entitled "Restrictive and Non-restrictive Modifiers" for information on how to use punctuation with relative pronouns.

Punctuation – Avoiding the Parenthetical

> Parentheticals should normally not be used to add extra information to a sentence.

Commas should be used, where possible. Alternatively, two sentences should be written.

INCORRECT: The car overturned on the motorway and then rolled down the embankment after the driver (because of drinking beforehand) lost control of the vehicle.

CORRECT: Because of drinking beforehand, the driver of the car lost control of the vehicle, which overturned on motorway and then rolled down the embankment.

CORRECT: The car overturned on the motorway and then rolled down the embankment after the driver lost control of the vehicle. The accident happened because he had been drinking beforehand.

Punctuation – Using the Apostrophe for Possessive Forms

Apostrophe placement depends upon whether a word is singular or plural.

For the singular form, the apostrophe should be placed before the "s".

SINGULAR: Our team's performance was poor at the match last night.

For the plural form, the apostrophe should be placed after the letter "s".

PLURAL: Both teams' performances were poor at the match last night.

Remember that the apostrophe is used in sentences like those above in order to show possession.

Do not use the apostrophe unnecessarily.

CORRECT: The dates for the events are 22 June and 5 July.

INCORRECT: The date's for the events are 22 June and 5 July.

INCORRECT: The dates' for the events are 22 June and 5 July.

Punctuation – Using Colons and Semicolons

> Colons (:) should be used when giving a list of items. Semicolons (;) should be used to join independent clauses.

COLON: The shop is offering discounts on the following items: DVDs, books and magazines.

SEMICOLON: I thought I would live in this city forever; then I lost my job.

Please see the section entitled "Punctuation and Independent Clauses" for more information on joining clauses.

Punctuation – Using Commas with Dates and Locations

> Commas should be used after the year in dates. Commas should also be used after towns, cities and countries.

DATES: On 2 September 1976, my mother was born.

LOCATIONS: Located in London, England, Big Ben is a major landmark.

Punctuation – Using Commas for Items in a Series

> When using "and" and "or" for more than two items in a series, be sure to omit the comma before the words "and" and "or".

CORRECT: You need to bring a tent, sleeping bag and torch.

INCORRECT: You need to bring a tent, sleeping bag, and torch.

Notice the omission of the comma after the word "bag" and before the word "and" in the series.

CORRECT: Students can call, write a letter or send an email.

INCORRECT: Students can call, write a letter, or send an email.

Notice the omission of the comma after the word "letter" and before the word "or" in the series.

Punctuation and Independent Clauses – Avoiding Run-On Sentences

> Run-on sentences are those that use commas to join independent clauses together, instead of correctly using the full stop.

An independent clause contains a grammatical subject and verb. It therefore can stand alone as its own sentence.

The first word of the independent clause should begin with a capital letter, and the clause should be preceded by a full stop.

CORRECT: I thought I would live in this city forever. Then I lost my job.

INCORRECT: I thought I would live in this city forever, then I lost my job.

"Then I lost my job" is a complete sentence. It has a grammatical subject (I) and a verb (lost). The independent clause must be preceded by a full stop, and the first word of the new sentence must begin with a capital letter.

Alternatively, an appropriate conjunction can be used to join the independent clauses:

I thought I would live in this city forever, and then I lost my job.

Restrictive and Non-restrictive Modifiers

> Restrictive modifiers are clauses or phrases that provide essential information that is needed in order to identify the grammatical subject.

Restrictive modifiers should not be preceded by a comma.

Example: My sister who lives in Manchester is a good swimmer.

In this case, the speaker has more than one sister, and she is identifying which sister she is talking about by giving the essential information "who lives in Manchester".

On the other hand, a non-restrictive modifier is a clause or phrase that provides extra information about a grammatical subject in a sentence. A non-restrictive modifier must be preceded by a comma.

Non-restrictive modifiers are also known as non-essential modifiers.

Example: My sister, who lives in Manchester, is a good swimmer.

In this case, the speaker has only one sister. Therefore, the information about her sister's city of residence is not essential in order to identify which sister she is talking about. So, the words "who lives in Manchester" form a non-restrictive modifier.

Sentence Fragments

> A sentence fragment is a group of words that does not express a complete train of thought.

CORRECT: I like Christine because she is so nice.

INCORRECT: I like Christine. Because she is so nice.

In the second example, "because she is so nice" is not a complete thought. This idea needs to be joined with the previous clause in order to be grammatically correct.

Subject-Verb Agreement

> Subjects must agree with verbs in number. Be careful with singulars and plurals.

Subject-verb agreement can be confusing when there are intervening words in a sentence.

CORRECT: The flowers in the pots in the garden grow quickly.

INCORRECT: The flowers in the pots in the garden grows quickly.

The grammatical subject in the above sentence is "flowers", not "garden", so the plural form of the verb (*grow*) needs to be used.

CORRECT: Each person in the groups of students needs to pay attention to the instructions.

INCORRECT: Each person in the groups of students need to pay attention to the instructions.

The grammatical subject in the above sentence is "each person", not "students". "Each" is singular and therefore requires the singular form of the verb (*needs*).

Now try the grammar exercises on the next page.

Grammar and Punctuation Exercises

Each of the sentences below has problems with grammar and punctuation. Find the errors in the sentences and correct them. You may wish to refer to the advice in the previous section as you do the exercise. The answers are provided on the page following the exercises.

1) I haven't seen her or her sister. Since they went away to college.

2) People who like to get up early in the morning in order to drink more coffee is likely to become easily tired in the afternoon.

3) Hanging from the knob on the bedroom door, Tom thought the new shirt was his favourite.

4) I ran across the street to speak to her, then she surprised me by saying that she had bought a new car.

5) Its common for a magazine to have better sales if it mentions computers, handhelds, or other new technology on it's cover.

6) Each student in the class who will take the series of exams on advanced mathematics need to study in advance.

7) Their are several reasons why there having problems with they're children.

8) You have to work hard to succeed at university, so each and every student need to devote time to their studies.

9) On 4 August 1975 the highest-ever temperature was reached in Edinburgh Scotland at 31.4° C.

10) Before leaving the building at night, please be sure to check the following – the lights, the locks, and them storage lockers on the second floor.

11) Student's motivation levels are usually higher when they need to study for final exams.

12) Your phone call (which I told you not to make) interrupted me during an important meeting.

Grammar and Punctuation Exercises – Answers

1) I haven't seen her or her sister since they went away to college.

2) People who like to get up early in the morning in order to drink more coffee are likely to become easily tired in the afternoon.

3) Hanging from the knob on the bedroom door, the new shirt was Tom's favourite.

4) I ran across the street to speak to her. Then she surprised me by saying that she had bought a new car.

5) It's common for a magazine to have better sales if it mentions computers, handhelds or other new technology on its cover.

6) Each student in the class who will take the series of exams on advanced mathematics needs to study in advance.

7) There are several reasons why they're having problems with their children.

8) Students have to work hard to succeed at university, so each and every student needs to devote time to his or her studies.

9) On 4 August 1975, the highest-ever temperature was reached in Edinburgh, Scotland, at 31.4° C.

10) Before leaving the building at night, please be sure to check the following: the lights, the locks and those storage lockers on the second floor.

11) Students' motivation levels are usually higher when they need to study for final exams.

12) Your phone call, which I told you not to make, interrupted me during an important meeting.

PART 3 – IELTS LANGUAGE PRACTICE

How to Use Phrases, Clauses and Cohesive Devices to Develop Your Sentences

In order to perform well on the IELTS writing test, you will need to write essays that have advanced and developed sentence structures.

Sentence linking words, sometimes called cohesive devices, are words and phrases that are used in order to combine short sentences together to create more complex sentence structures.

Sentence linking words and phrases fall into three categories: sentence linkers, phrase linkers and subordinators.

In order to understand how to use these types of sentence linking words and phrases correctly, you will need to know some basics of English grammar.

The basic grammatical principles for these concepts are explained in this section. Be sure to study the examples carefully before you attempt the exercises in the following section of the study guide.

TYPE 1 – SENTENCE LINKERS:

Sentence linkers are used to link two complete sentences together. A complete sentence is one that has a grammatical subject and a verb. Sentence linkers are usually placed at the beginning of a sentence and are followed by a comma.

They can also be preceded by a semicolon and followed by a comma when joining two sentences together. When doing so, the first letter of the first word of the second sentence must not be capitalised.

Sentence linker examples:

You need to enjoy your time at university. *However*, you should still study hard.

You need to enjoy your time at university; *however*, you should still study hard.

In the examples above, the grammatical subject of the first sentence is "you" and the verb is "need to enjoy".

In the second sentence, "you" is the grammatical subject and "should study" is the verb.

TYPE 2 – PHRASE LINKERS:

In order to understand the difference between phrase linkers and sentence linkers, you must first be able to distinguish a sentence from a phrase.

A phrase linker must be followed by a phrase, while a sentence linker must be followed by a sentence. The basic distinction between phrases and sentences is that phrases do not have both grammatical subjects and verbs, while sentences contain grammatical subjects and verbs.

Here are some examples of phrases:

Her beauty and grace

Life's little problems

A lovely summer day in the month of June

Working hard

Being desperate for money

Note that the last two phrases above use the –ing form, known in these instances as the present participle.

Present participle phrases, which are often used to modify nouns or pronouns, are sometimes placed at the beginning of sentences as introductory phrases.

Here are some examples of sentences:

Mary worked all day long.

My sister lives in Newcastle.

Wintertime is brutal in Inverness.

"Mary", "my sister" and "wintertime" are the grammatical subjects of the above sentences.

Remember that verbs are words that show action or states of being, so "worked", "lives" and "is" are the verbs in the three sentences above.

Look at the examples that follow:

Phrase linker example 1 – no comma:

He received a promotion *because of* his dedication to the job.

"His dedication to the job" is a noun phrase.

Phrase linker example 2 – with comma:

Because of his dedication to the job, he received a promotion.

When the sentence begins with the phrase linker, we classify the sentence as an inverted sentence.

Notice that you will need to place a comma between the two parts of the sentence when it is inverted.

TYPE 3 – SUBORDINATORS:

Subordinators must be followed by an independent clause. Subordinators cannot be followed by a phrase.

The two clauses of a subordinated sentence must be separated by a comma.

The structure of independent clauses is similar to that of sentences because independent clauses contain a grammatical subject and a verb.

Subordinator examples:

Although he worked hard, he failed to make his business profitable.

He failed to make his business profitable, *although* he worked hard.

There are two clauses: "He worked hard" and "he failed to make his business profitable".

The grammatical subjects in each clause are the words "he", while the verbs are "worked" and "failed".

Now look at the sentence linking words and phrases below. Note which ones are sentence linkers, which ones are phrase linkers and which ones are subordinators.

Then refer to the rules above to remember the grammatical principles for sentence linkers, phrase linkers and subordinators.

Sentence linkers for giving additional information

further

furthermore

apart from this

what is more

in addition

additionally

in the same way

moreover

Sentence linkers for giving examples

for example

for instance

in this case

in particular

more precisely

namely

in brief

in short

Sentence linkers for stating the obvious

obviously

clearly

naturally

of course

surely

after all

Sentence linkers for giving generalisations

in general

on the whole

as a rule

for the most part

generally speaking

in most cases

Sentence linkers for stating causes and effects

thus

accordingly

hence

therefore

in that case

under those circumstances

as a result

for this reason

as a consequence

consequently

in effect

Sentence linkers for concession or unexpected results

however

nevertheless

meanwhile

Sentence linkers for giving conclusions

finally

to conclude

lastly

in conclusion

Sentence linkers for contrast

on the other hand

on the contrary

alternatively

rather

Sentence linkers for paraphrasing or restating

in other words

that is to say

that is

Sentence linkers for showing similarity

similarly

in the same way

likewise

Phrase linkers for giving additional information

besides

in addition to

Phrase linkers for stating causes and effects

because of

due to

owing to

Phrase linkers for concession or unexpected results

despite

in spite of

Phrase linkers for comparison

compared to

like

Phrase linkers for contrast

in contrast to

instead of

rather than

without

Subordinators

although

as

because

but

due to the fact that

even though

since

so

once

unless

until

when

whereas

while

not only . . . but also

Time words that can be used both as phrase linkers and subordinators

after

before

Special cases

yet – "Yet" can be used as both a subordinator and as a sentence linker.

in order to – "In order to" must be followed by the base form of the verb.

thereby – "Thereby" must be followed by the present participle.

We will look at the present participle and base forms in the following exercises.

Sentence Development Exercises

Look at the pairs of sentences in the exercises below. Make new sentences, using the phrase linkers, sentence linkers and subordinators provided. In many cases, you will need to create one single sentence from the two sentences provided. You may need to change or delete some of the words in the original sentences.

Exercise 1:

The temperature was quite high yesterday.

It really didn't feel that hot outside.

Write new sentences beginning as follows:

a) In spite of . . .

Hint: You need to change the form of the verb "was" in answer (a).

b) The temperature . . .

You need to include the word "nevertheless" in answer (b). Be careful with punctuation and capitalisation in your answer.

Exercise 2:

Our star athlete didn't receive a gold medal in the Olympics.

He had trained for competition for several years in advance.

Write new sentences beginning as follows:

a) Our star athlete . . . .

Answer (a) should contain the word "although".

b) Despite . . .

Exercise 3:

There are acrimonious relationships within our extended family.

Our immediate family decided to go away on holiday at the end of December to avoid these conflicts.

Write new sentences beginning as follows:

a) Because of . . .

b) Because . . .

c) Due to the fact that . . .

Exercise 4:

My best friend had been feeling extremely sick for several days.

She refused to see the doctor.

Write new sentences beginning as follows:

a) My best friend . . .

Answer (a) should contain the word "however".

b) My best friend . . .

Answer (b) should contain the word "but".

Be careful with capitalisation and punctuation in your answers.

Exercise 5:

He generally doesn't like drinking alcohol.

He will do so on social occasions.

Write new sentences beginning as follows:

a) While . . .

b) He generally . . .

Answer (b) should contain the word "yet".

Exercise 6:

The government's policies failed to stimulate spending and expand economic growth.

The country slipped further into recession.

Write new sentences beginning as follows:

a) The government's policies . . .

Answer (a) should contain the word "thus".

b) The government's policies . . .

Answer (b) should contain the word "so".

Exercise 7:

Students may attend certain classes without fulfilling a prerequisite.

Students are advised of the benefit of taking at least one non-required introductory course.

Write new sentences beginning as follows:

a) Even though . . .

b) Students may attend . . .

Answer (b) should contain the phrase "apart from this".

Exercise 8:

There have been advances in technology and medical science.

Infant mortality rates have declined substantially in recent years.

Write new sentences beginning as follows:

a) Owing to . . .

b) Since . . .

Exercise 9:

It was the most expensive restaurant in town.

It had rude staff and provided the worst service.

Write new sentences beginning as follows:

a) It was the most . . .

Answer (a) should contain the word "besides".

b) In addition to . . .

Exercise 10:

Now try to combine these three sentences:

The judge did not punish the criminal justly.

He decided to grant a lenient sentence.

He did not send out a message to deter potential offenders in the future.

Write new sentences as follows:

a) Instead of . . . and thereby . . .

b) Rather than . . . in order to . . .

Before you attempt your answer, look for the cause and effect relationships among the three sentences. In other words, which event came first? Which ones were second and third in the chain of events? Also be careful with punctuation in your answers.

Sentence Development Exercises – Answers & Explanations

Exercise 1:

Answer (a): In spite of the temperature being quite high yesterday, it really didn't feel that hot outside.

The words "in spite of" are a phrase linker, not a sentence linker.

That is to say, "in spite of" needs to be followed by a phrase, not a clause.

The verb "was" needs to be changed to "being" in order to form a present participle phrase.

Present participle phrases are made by using the –ing form of the verb.

We will see this construction again in some of the following answers.

Answer (b): There are two possible answers.

The temperature was quite high yesterday. Nevertheless, it really didn't feel that hot outside.

The temperature was quite high yesterday; nevertheless, it really didn't feel that hot outside.

"Nevertheless" is a sentence linker. As such, it needs to be used to begin a new sentence.

Alternatively, the semicolon can be used to join the original sentences. If the semicolon is used, the first letter of the word following it must not be capitalised.

Exercise 2:

Answer (a): Our star athlete didn't receive a gold medal in the Olympics, although he had trained for competition for several years in advance

"Although" is a subordinator, so the two sentences can be combined without any changes.

Answer (b): Despite having trained for competition for several years in advance, our star athlete didn't receive a gold medal in the Olympics.

"Despite" is a phrase linker. As we have seen in answer (a) of exercise 1 above, phrase linkers need to be followed by phrases, not clauses.

The two parts of the sentence are inverted, and the verb "had" needs to be changed to "having" to make the present participle form.

Exercise 3:

Answer (a): Because of acrimonious relationships within our extended family, our immediate family decided to go away on holiday at the end of December to avoid these conflicts.

"Because of" is a phrase linker. As such, the subject and verb (there are) need to be removed from the original sentence in order to form a phrase.

Answer (b): Because there are acrimonious relationships within our extended family, our immediate family decided to go away on holiday at the end of December to avoid these conflicts.

Answer (c): Due to the fact that there are acrimonious relationships within our extended family, our immediate family decided to go away on holiday at the end of December to avoid these conflicts.

"Because" and "due to the fact that" are subordinators, so no changes to the original sentences are required.

The phrase "to avoid these conflicts" can be omitted since this idea is already implied by the words "acrimonious relationships".

Exercise 4:

Answer (a): There are two possible answers.

My best friend had been feeling extremely sick for several days. However, she refused to see the doctor.

My best friend had been feeling extremely sick for several days; however, she refused to see the doctor.

Like "nevertheless" in exercise 1, the word "however" is a sentence linker. Remember that sentence linkers need to be used at the beginning of a new sentence.

Alternatively, the semicolon can be used to join the original sentences. If the semicolon is used, "however" must not begin with a capital letter and needs to be followed by a comma.

Answer (b): My best friend had been feeling extremely sick for several days, but she refused to see the doctor.

"But" is a subordinator, so the two sentences can be combined without any changes.

Exercise 5:

Answer (a): While he generally doesn't like drinking alcohol, he will do so on social occasions.

Like the word "although", the word "while" is a subordinator, so no changes to the original sentences are needed.

Answer (b): "Yet" can be used as both a subordinator and as a sentence linker, so there are three possible answers in this instance.

When used as a sentence linker, the sentence construction is similar to the sentences containing nevertheless" from exercise 1 and "however" from exercise 4.

Accordingly, the two following sentences are possible answers:

He doesn't like drinking alcohol. Yet, he will do so on social occasions.

He doesn't like drinking alcohol; yet, he will do so on social occasions.

A third possible answer is to use "yet" as a subordinator.

He doesn't like drinking alcohol, yet he will do so on social occasions.

The difference is that the third sentence places slightly less emphasis on the particular occasions in which he will drink than the other two sentences.

Exercise 6:

Answer (a): "Thus" is a sentence linker, so there are two possible answers.

a) The government's policies failed to stimulate spending and expand economic growth. Thus, the country slipped further into recession.

a) The government's policies failed to stimulate spending and expand economic growth; thus, the country slipped further into recession.

Answer (b): The government's policies failed to stimulate spending and expand economic growth, so the country slipped further into recession.

"So" is a subordinator. The two sentences may therefore be joined without any changes.

Exercise 7:

Answer (a): There are two possible answers.

Even though students may attend certain classes without fulfilling a prerequisite, they are advised of the benefit of taking at least one non-required introductory course.

Even though students are advised of the benefit of taking at least one non-required introductory course, they may attend certain classes without fulfilling a prerequisite.

"Even though" is a subordinator, so no changes are needed. It is advisable to change the word "students" to the pronoun "they" on the second part of the new sentence in order to avoid repetition.

The order or the clauses may be changed in the new sentence since there is no cause and effect relationship between the two original sentences.

Answer (b): There are two possible answers.

Students may attend certain classes without fulfilling a prerequisite. Apart from this, they are advised of the benefit of taking at least one non-required introductory course.

Students may attend certain classes without fulfilling a prerequisite; apart from this, they are advised of the benefit of taking at least one non-required introductory course.

"Apart from this" is a sentence linker, so it needs to be used at the beginning of a separate sentence.

Exercise 8:

Answer (a): Owing to advances in technology and medical science, infant mortality rates have declined substantially in recent years.

"Owing to" is a phrase linker that shows cause and effect. In this case the cause is advances in technology and medical science, and the effect or result is the decline in infant mortality rates.

Since "owing to" is a phrase linker, the grammatical subject of the original sentence (there) and the verb (have been) are removed when creating the new sentence.

Answer (b): Since there have been advances in technology and medical science, infant mortality rates have declined substantially in recent years.

"Since" is a subordinator, so you can combine the sentences without making any changes.

Remember to use the comma between the two parts of the sentence because the clauses have been inverted.

Exercise 9:

Answer (a): It was the most expensive restaurant in town, besides having rude staff and providing the worst service.

"Besides" is a phrase linker, so use the present participle form of both verbs in the second original sentence. Accordingly, "had" becomes "having" and "provide" becomes "providing".

Answer (b): There are two possible answers.

In addition to being the most expensive restaurant in town, it had rude staff and provided the worst service.

In addition to having rude staff and providing the worst service, it was the most expensive restaurant in town.

"In addition to" is a phrase linker, so the present participle forms are used in the phrase containing this word.

The order of the original sentences can be changed since there is no cause and effect relationship between these ideas.

Exercise 10:

Answer (a): Instead of punishing the criminal justly and thereby sending out a message to deter potential offenders in the future, the judge decided to grant a lenient sentence.

Answer (b): Rather than punishing the criminal justly in order to send out a message to deter potential offenders in the future, the judge decided to grant a lenient sentence.

As you will see, answers A and B are somewhat similar in their construction.

"Instead of" and "rather than" need to be used with the present particle form (punishing).

"Thereby" must be followed by the present participle form (sending). However, "in order to" needs to take the base form of the verb (send). The base form is the verb before any change has been made to it, like making the –ed or –ing forms. The following are examples of base forms of verbs: eat, sleep, work, play.

PART 4 – TASK 1 ESSAYS

As stated at the beginning of this book, task 1 of the IELTS Academic Writing Test is a data analysis task.

In order to do well on this task, you will need to know how to interpret and write about various types of data.

What are the different types of data representation?

The data that you will see on IELTS writing task 1 can be represented in various ways. You may see any of the following on task 1:

- Pie charts
- Bar graphs
- Line graphs
- Tables

Analysing the data before you write

Think about the data and analyse it before you begin to write.

You might find it helpful to ask yourself the following questions:

- What is being represented?
- What is represented in the x axis? (The x axis is at the bottom of a chart or graph.)
- What is represented in the y axis? (The y axis is at the left-hand side of a chart or graph.)

How to Structure the Task 1 Essay

IELTS academic writing task 1 asks you to write a report on the data, but it will not give you any instructions about what specific aspects of the data you should mention in your response to the task.

Students sometimes find this aspect of the task confusing, especially since there are often many things on which to comment in the data.

As a general rule of thumb, you can think of task 1 as having three parts:

1. Introducing the data
2. Reporting on significant details
3. Describing overall trends

The first part of your task 1 response should always be the introduction. The significant details are usually discussed before moving on to describe the overall trends.

Placing the three parts of the report in this order is particularly useful when there are significant aspects that appear to have affected the overall trends.

However, you can also describe the overall trends before you describe the significant details.

How to Introduce the Data

Your first one or two sentences should briefly summarise what the graph or table represents. Do not repeat phrases from the title of the graph or from the exam question. For example, consider the following table:

Instructions: The table below shows the number of union members per year for Oxfordshire, Wiltshire, Somerset and the Remaining Counties in England from 1994 to 2014. Please analyse the data and comment on its significant characteristics.

Union Members in Oxfordshire, Wiltshire, Somerset and Remaining Counties				
Year	Oxfordshire	Wiltshire	Somerset	Remaining Counties
1994	2,365	1,981	3,687	52,187
1999	1,987	1,945	3,522	48,233
2004	1,784	1,915	3,623	51,505
2009	1,801	1,899	3,547	50,689
2014	1,121	1,892	3,601	49,117

Your task 1 response should not begin like this:

The table shows the number of union members per year for Oxfordshire, Wiltshire, Somerset and the Remaining Counties in England from 1994 to 2014.

The sentence above is taken exactly from the information for the task. In other words, you should paraphrase the information in the task description, rather than repeating it word for word.

A possible paraphrase for the introduction might look like this:

The data reflected in the chart represents union memberships for three English counties and for the remainder of England for the period 1994 to 2014. The amounts of union memberships are reported every five years for the twenty-year period shown on the chart.

How to Select and Comment on Significant Details

You should write two or three sentences about the significant details of the data.

Bear in mind that you may need to compare and contrast some of the details.

Let's look at our chart again.

Union Members in Oxfordshire, Wiltshire, Somerset and Remaining Counties				
Year	Oxfordshire	Wiltshire	Somerset	Remaining Counties
1994	2,365	1,981	3,687	52,187
1999	1,987	1,945	3,522	48,233
2004	1,784	1,915	3,623	51,505
2009	1,801	1,899	3,547	50,689
2014	1,121	1,892	3,601	49,117

In order to determine which details are the most significant, you should look to see which years are the highest and the lowest for each group. You should also determine if there is any dramatic change for any group in any particular year.

Here is a possible commentary on the significant details:

Union membership in Oxfordshire fell to its lowest point in 2014, experiencing a significant drop in that year compared to 2009. However, the total for Wiltshire showed only a slight dip over the same five-year period. Both Somerset and the remaining counties had their highest memberships in 1994, followed by their second highest memberships in 2004.

How to Describe Overall Trends

Your next two sentences should give general information about the data. You should therefore look at each of the groups represented in the table and determine whether the amounts for each group have increased, decreased, remained more or less stable, or fluctuated.

Union Members in Oxfordshire, Wiltshire, Somerset and Remaining Counties				
Year	Oxfordshire	Wiltshire	Somerset	Remaining Counties
1994	2,365	1,981	3,687	52,187
1999	1,987	1,945	3,522	48,233
2004	1,784	1,915	3,623	51,505
2009	1,801	1,899	3,547	50,689
2014	1,121	1,892	3,601	49,117

Sample response on overall trends:

In terms of overall trends for each county, union membership in Oxfordshire has declined steadily since 1994. Membership in Wiltshire and Somerset remained more or less constant over these twenty years, but the amount of union members in other counties in England fluctuated considerably over the two decades represented in the data displayed in the chart.

Task 1 – Sample Response

Finally, we need to combine our three components together to get our report for task 1.

The data reflected in the chart represents union memberships for three English counties and for the remainder of England for the period 1994 to 2014. The amounts of union memberships are reported every five years for the twenty-year period shown on the chart. Union membership in Oxfordshire fell to its lowest point in 2014, experiencing a significant drop in that year compared to 2009. However, the total for Wiltshire showed only a slight dip over the same five-year period. Both Somerset and the remaining counties had their highest memberships in 1994, followed by their second highest memberships in 2004. In terms of overall trends for each area, union membership in Oxfordshire has declined steadily since 1994. Membership in Wiltshire and Somerset remained more or less constant over these twenty years, but the amount of union members in other counties in England fluctuated considerably over the two decades represented in the data displayed in the chart.

Useful Words and Phrases for Writing Task 1

The following words are phrases can be used in IELTS writing task 1. For more examples on how to use these words and phrases, please see the sample essays at the end of this book.

Useful words and phrases:

Rise

Increase

Fall

Drop

Decline

Peak

Dip

Fluctuate

Reach a peak

Rise to the highest point

Fall to the lowest point

Remain constant

Remain the same

Remain stable

Remain steady

Plateau

In contrast to

Compared to

Similarly

Likewise

In the same way

Just as

Although

But

However

While

Considerable / Considerably

Dramatic / Dramatically

Gradual / Gradually

Relative / Relatively

Sharp / Sharply

Significant / Significantly

Slight / Slightly

Substantial / Substantially

Sudden / Suddenly

PART 5 – TASK 2 ESSAYS

Task 2 Essay Structure:

Most teachers agree that the best IELTS task 2 essays follow a four or five paragraph format. This format will help to insure that your essay is well-organised.

This format also helps you write longer and more developed essays that will achieve the 250 word requirement.

The five paragraph essay is organised as follows:

Paragraph 1 – This paragraph is the introduction to your essay. It should include a thesis statement that clearly indicates your main idea. It should also give the reader an overview of your supporting points.

Paragraph 2 – The second paragraph is where you elaborate on your first supporting point. It is normally recommended that you state your strongest and most persuasive point in this paragraph.

Paragraph 3 – You should elaborate on your main idea in the third paragraph by providing a second supporting point.

Paragraph 4 – You should mention your third supporting point in the fourth paragraph. This can be the supporting point that you feel to be the weakest.

Paragraph 5 – In the fifth and final paragraph of the essay, you should make your conclusion. The conclusion should reiterate your supporting points and sum up your position.

The four paragraph essay will follow the same structure as above, with paragraphs 2 and 3 elaborating two key supporting points and paragraph 4 stating the conclusion.

If you decide to put four paragraphs in your essay instead of five, each paragraph should be longer and slightly more detailed than that of a five paragraph essay.

We will illustrate the five paragraph essay format in our sample essay in the subsequent units of this study guide.

Creating Effective Thesis Statements

What is a thesis statement?

A thesis statement is a sentence that asserts the main idea of your essay. The thesis statement is placed in the first paragraph of your essay. Most task 2 essays on the IELTS will be on debatable or contentious topics. You will not need to write about both sides of the argument for the given topic. You only need to state which side of the argument you support and give reasons for your viewpoint.

Write it early

It is important to draft your thesis statement early in the writing process so that your writing has focus. However, be prepared to go back and edit your thesis statement after you have finished the main body of your essay.

Keep it focused

Remember that the best thesis statements are those that contain a central idea that will serve to narrow the focus of the essay and control the flow ideas within it. As such, a thesis statement should not be too general or vague.

The "Assertion + Reason" Structure

A good structure for the thesis statement is to think of it in terms of an assertion plus a reason or explanation. This structure is better than just giving your assertion or opinion on its own because your explanation indicates the direction that your writing is going to take.

In addition, the "assertion + reason" structure will result in a thesis statement that contains more words and which is usually richer grammatically and structurally.

Bearing these tips in mind, you should now complete the thesis statement exercise on the following pages.

Thesis Statement – Exercise

Now look at the essay topic below and write a focused thesis statement, using the "Assertion + Reason" thesis statement structure.

Most people have access to computers and mobile phones on a daily basis, making email and text messaging extremely popular. While some argue that email and texting are now the most convenient forms of personal communication, others believe that electronic communication technology is often used inappropriately. Write an essay for an audience of educated adults in which you take a position on this topic. Be sure to provide reasons and examples to support your viewpoint.

Your thesis statement:

Thesis Statement – Answer to Exercise

Suggested answer:

Modern forms of communication such as electronic mail and SMS messaging can cause problems with personal relationships because of three main shortcomings with these media: their impersonal nature, their inability to capture tone and sarcasm and their easy accessibility at times of anger.

Analysis:

The assertion is that "Modern forms of communication such as electronic mail and SMS messaging can cause problems with personal relationships".

The reasons are "their impersonal nature, their inability to capture tone and sarcasm and their easy accessibility at times of anger".

The essay will be focused because it will have three main body paragraphs, which will discuss each of the reasons provided.

Writing the Introduction

What is the purpose of the introduction?

The purpose of your introduction is to give a brief statement of your point of view and to provide an overview of your supporting points.

What can I include in my introduction?

You can include a vivid example, an interesting fact, a paradoxical statement or even a supporting anecdote in your introduction.

When should I write the introduction?

Although it is advisable to write your thesis statement before beginning your main body, you can often go back and write the remainder of the introduction after you have finished the body paragraphs and conclusion. That is because sometimes it is easier to introduce your essay after you have already written it and developed your points.

What is the structure of the introduction?

You can think of the essay introduction like a funnel: wide at the top and narrow at the bottom. In other words, start off your introduction in a general but interesting way, and then narrow it down to your main idea and specific supporting points.

Remember that the introduction announces your main idea and supporting points, while your main body develops them.

Writing the Introduction – Exercise

Look at our previous essay topic again and write an introduction for your essay. Remember to include a clear and focused thesis statement at the end of your introduction. A sample answer is provided on the following page.

Most people have access to computers and mobile phones on a daily basis, making email and text messaging extremely popular. While some argue that email and texting are now the most convenient forms of personal communication, others believe that electronic communication technology is often used inappropriately. Write an essay for an audience of educated adults in which you take a position on this topic. Be sure to provide reasons and examples to support your viewpoint.

Your introduction:

Writing the Introduction – Answer

Suggested answer:

There is no disputing the fact that email and SMS technologies have made our lives easier in a variety of ways. Nevertheless, many of us will have had the experience of falling out with a friend or loved one over an email or text message whose content was poorly written or misconstrued. Clearly, there are certain drawbacks to emails and texts since electronic messaging cannot capture the nuances and subtleties of verbal communication. Modern forms of communication such as electronic mail and SMS messaging can cause problems with personal relationships because of three main shortcomings with these media: their impersonal nature, their inability to capture tone and sarcasm and their easy accessibility at times of anger.

Analysis:

The first sentence describes the effect of communication technology on daily life in general.

The second sentence provides an interesting anecdote because the account of having a disagreement with a loved one about the content of an email message is a universal experience.

The third sentence logically connects the example of miscommunication to the thesis statement.

The fourth sentence of the introduction is the thesis statement, which also contains the supporting points.

Organising the Main Body

Each paragraph of your main body should consist of the following elements:

1. A topic sentence which concisely states the supporting point that you are going to discuss in the paragraph.
2. Well-written and complex sentences that elaborate on your supporting points through reasons and examples.
3. The use of subordination and linking words in order to create a variety of different types of sentence construction.

You may wish to write the body of the paragraph before writing your topic sentence for it because sometimes it is easier to sum up the main point of the paragraph after you have written it.

For this reason, we will next look at elaboration of supporting points and writing the main body sentences, before turning our attention to topic sentences.

Elaboration in the Body Paragraphs

<u>What is an elaborating idea?</u>

Elaborating ideas include both explanations and examples. Providing clear examples to support your points is extremely important because it helps to make your essay more persuasive.

Each of your main body paragraphs should contain an example that supports your line of argument.

You should elaborate on and explain your example in order to make your essay persuasive.

<u>How do elaborating ideas help to raise my score?</u>

Elaboration lengthens your essay and gives you more opportunities to demonstrate higher-level grammar, complex sentence construction and academic vocabulary.

These criteria (grammar, construction and vocabulary) are considered when the examiner gives your essay an IELTS band score.

<u>How many elaborating ideas should I have in each paragraph?</u>

You can have two or three elaborating ideas in each body paragraph.

How do I link my elaborating ideas to one another?

You should seamlessly link your elaborating points together to make a coherent paragraph. This is the function of linking words and subordination, which we have seen in Part 3 of the study guide.

How do I come up with elaborating ideas for each supporting point?

Perhaps the best way to elaborate on your supporting points is to take each of the supporting points that you are going to talk about in your main body paragraphs, place them as headings on a piece of scratch paper, and make a list of examples and explanations under each heading.

We will have a look at how to do this in the following exercise.

Elaboration of Supporting Points – Exercise

Let's turn our attention to our sample essay on email and text communication.

Here is the introduction again for ease of reference:

> There is no disputing the fact that email and SMS technologies have made our lives easier in a variety of ways. Nevertheless, many of us will have had the experience of falling out with a friend or loved one over an email or text message whose content was poorly written or misconstrued. Clearly, there are certain drawbacks to emails and texts since electronic messaging cannot capture the nuances and subtleties of verbal communication. Modern forms of communication such as electronic mail and SMS messaging can cause problems with personal relationships because of three main shortcomings with these media: their impersonal nature, their inability to capture tone and sarcasm and their easy accessibility at times of anger.

This will be a five paragraph essay, so in your first body paragraph you need to elaborate on the impersonal nature of electronic communication. Your second body paragraph will elaborate on how emails and texts cannot convey tone and sarcasm.

The third paragraph will talk about the danger of having an accessible messaging service during times of high emotion.

Exercise – Now try to make a list of the ideas you are going to use as elaboration for each of your main body paragraphs. Sample responses are provided on the following page.

Elaboration – Body Paragraph 1:

Elaboration – Body Paragraph 2:

Elaboration – Body Paragraph 3:

Elaboration of Supporting Points – Answer to Exercise

Elaboration – Body Paragraph 1:

Elaborate on the impersonal nature of electronic communication

- Email is practical, but not always appropriate. Example: informing someone about a death
- No human contact – can be seen as cold or shallow – not like talking on phone or in person

Elaboration – Body Paragraph 2:

Emails and texts cannot convey tone and sarcasm

- It is possible for sarcastic comments to be taken literally
- Message clear to sender, but tone of emotion is conveyed by voice
- Without tone, may come across as demanding, indifferent, etc.

Elaboration – Body Paragraph 3:

The danger of having an accessible messaging service during times of high emotion

- Examples: breaking up with someone by text; firing someone by email
- Easy to send a message quickly when angry – can hurt relationships – waiting and thinking requires self-control & discipline

Writing the Main Body Paragraphs – Exercise

We had a look at brainstorming ideas for your main body paragraphs in a previous section of this study guide.

We will now return to the ideas we developed in that section and write the paragraphs of the main body of our essay.

We will also need the skills we have practiced in the "IELTS Language Practice" section in Part 3 of the book in order to use sentence linking words and subordination to write in an organised way.

Remember that while sentence linking words and subordination are important because they give an essay cohesion and structure, you should avoid using a sentence linker or subordinator in every sentence of your essay. That is because you should use a variety of sentence patterns in your essay.

Accordingly, some of the sentences in our model answer will have linking words and subordinators, although others will not.

Within each exercise, we reproduce our list of elaborating points for the body paragraphs for ease of reference.

Now write the sentences for main body paragraphs for essay task 2, excluding the topic sentence. Some words from the basic sentence structure of the sample response are provided in order to guide you. Refer to the lists above each exercise to help you. Write each new sentence in the order of the points provided

Main Body Paragraph 1:

Elaborate on the impersonal nature of electronic communication

- Email is practical, but not always appropriate. Example: informing someone about a death
- No human contact – can be seen as cold or shallow – not like talking on phone or in person

Sentence 1: Although email may be practical for . . . , electronic messaging would be remarkably inappropriate for . . .

Sentence 2: There is no direct human contact in . . . , and during times of loss or tragedy, human warmth . . .

Main Body Paragraph 2:

Emails and texts cannot convey tone and sarcasm

- It is possible for sarcastic comments to be taken literally
- Message clear to sender, but tone of emotion is conveyed by voice
- Without tone, may come across as demanding, indifferent, etc.

Sentence 1: For instance, it might be possible . . . of a sarcastic email message to . . .

Sentence 2: The tone of . . . may seem abundantly clear to . . . , but sarcastic or ironically humorous utterances can only . . .

Sentence 3: Without . . . , certain phrases in an email may . . .

Main Body Paragraph 3:

The danger of having an accessible messaging service during times of high emotion

- Examples: breaking up with someone by text; firing someone by email
- Easy to send a message quickly when angry – can hurt relationships – waiting and thinking requires self-control & discipline

Sentence 1: In this day and age, we have heard stories not only of . . . , but also of employers who . . .

Sentence 2: Unless the writer of the message has . . . before . . . , he or she might send a regrettable message that can . . .

Suggested Answers – Main Body Paragraphs

Sample Body Paragraph 1 (excluding topic sentence):

Although email may be practical for conveying straightforward information or facts, electronic messaging would be remarkably inappropriate for events like announcing a death. There is no direct human contact in emails and texts, and during times of loss or tragedy, human warmth and depth of emotion can only truly be conveyed through a phone call, or better still, by talking face to face.

Sample Body Paragraph 2 (excluding topic sentence):

For instance, it might be possible for the recipient of a sarcastic email message to take its contents literally. The tone of the message may seem abundantly clear to the person who sent it, but sarcastic or ironically humorous utterances can only really be communicated in speech through the tone and inflection of the voice. Without the aid of tone and inflection, certain phrases in an email may come across as demanding, indifferent or rude.

Sample Body Paragraph 3 (excluding topic sentence):

In this day and age, we have heard stories not only of personal break ups that have been conducted by text, but also of employers who fire their staff by email message. Unless the writer of the message has the discipline and self-control to give him or herself a period of reasoned contemplation before sending the communication, he or she might send a regrettable message that can cause irretrievable damage to a relationship.

Writing Clear and Concise Topic Sentences

Why are topic sentences important?

As the IELTS examiner reads each new paragraph of your essay, he or she will look for new ideas by searching for words and phrases that you have not used previously in your writing.

Each topic sentence should therefore paraphrase, *but not repeat word for word*, the supporting points in your thesis statement.

What is the purpose of a topic sentence?

You can think of the topic sentence as a summary of the content of a main body paragraph. The topic sentence serves two purposes.

First of all, it gives an overview of the content of the paragraph because it announces the topic that you are going to discuss.

Secondly, the topic sentence links back to the thesis statement since it is an elaboration of one of the supporting points that you have already cited at the beginning of the essay.

In this way, clear and concise topic sentences give your essay cohesion and coherence.

Is a topic sentence general or specific in its focus?

While the topic sentence is more specific than the thesis statement, the topic sentence should be more general than the elaboration that you are going to make in the paragraph.

In other words, in the same way that your introductory paragraph moves from a general idea to more specific ones, so too does each main body paragraph move from the more general supporting point that you mention in your topic sentence to the specific points that you raise in your elaboration.

How do I avoid repeating myself?

Remember that although your topic sentences point back to the thesis statement, you need to avoid using the exact same wording in your topic sentences as in your thesis statement.

For instance, if you refer to the "impersonal nature of electronic communication" in your thesis statement, your topic sentence should word this idea differently.

In this case, the phrase "impersonal nature of electronic communication" could be paraphrased by stating: "There is no direct human contact in email".

Where should a topic sentence be placed within the paragraph?

The most common position for the topic sentence is the first sentence of the paragraph.

In longer essays, it is possible to put a topic sentence as the second sentence of a paragraph if the paragraph's first sentence is transitional.

You can also delay the topic sentence until the end of the paragraph for emphasis, although for the sake of clarity, this is not recommended.

For the IELTS essay, you should plan to write two or three main body paragraphs, each of which have a topic sentence as their first sentence.

Topic Sentences – Exercise

Let's turn our attention to writing topic sentences for the main body paragraphs of our essay on email and text communication.

The topic sentence for your first body paragraph will mention the impersonal nature of electronic communication.

Your topic sentence for the second body paragraph will mention how the tone of emails and texts can be misunderstood.

The topic sentence of your third paragraph will talk about the danger of having a quick messaging service at hand when you are angry.

Exercise – Now try to write topic sentence for each of your main body paragraphs. Remember that the topic sentence needs to be specific for each supporting point, but general enough to introduce the paragraph as a whole. You may wish to refer back to what you have written thus far on the essay topic. Sample responses are provided on the next page.

Topic Sentence 1:

Topic Sentence 2:

Topic Sentence 3:

Topic Sentences – Answer to Exercise

Here are possible topic sentences for the three main body paragraphs.

Topic Sentence 1:

Depending upon the context, the recipient of an email or text message may consider this mode of communication to be insensitive or uncaring.

Analysis:

The phrase "their impersonal nature" from the thesis statement has been re-worded as "insensitive or uncaring".

Topic Sentence 2:

A further problem with emails and texts is that they do not always accurately express the tone which the writer has intended.

Analysis:

The idea of "their inability to capture tone and sarcasm" from the thesis statement has been paraphrased as "they do not always accurately express the tone which the writer has intended".

Topic Sentence 3:

The danger of having an accessible messaging service readily at hand during times of high emotion is another insidious problem with electronic media.

Analysis:

The phrase "their easy accessibility at times of anger" from the thesis statement has been expressed here as "readily at hand during times of high emotion".

Also note that the words "further" from topic sentence 2 and "another" from topic sentence 3 improve the flow of the essay by signalling that new ideas are being introduced in these paragraphs.

Writing the Conclusion

Conclusions for IELTS task 2 essays can consist of as few as two sentences, provided that the sentences are cohesive, coherent and well-constructed.

As in other parts of your essay, you will need to reiterate certain concepts in the conclusion, without repeating word for word what you have already written.

In particular, your conclusion should echo your introduction, without copying the exact phrases you have used at the start of your essay or in the body paragraphs.

You will continue to need linking words and phrases in the conclusion in order to give a good flow to your writing.

The final sentence of your conclusion can be used to give advice or to make a prediction about the future. This will give a forward-looking aspect to your essay and will help your writing to end on a strong note.

Writing the Conclusion – Exercise

Look at the underlined words from the introduction to the essay below. Then look at the sample conclusion and identify the words which paraphrase these concepts.

Finally, circle the linking words and phrases that are used in the sample conclusion.

Introduction:

There is no disputing the fact that <u>email and SMS technologies have made our lives easier in a variety of ways</u>. Nevertheless, many of us will have had the experience of falling out with a friend or loved one over an email or text message whose content was poorly written or misconstrued. Clearly, <u>there are certain drawbacks to emails and texts</u> since electronic messaging <u>cannot capture the nuances</u> and <u>subtleties of verbal communication</u>. Modern forms of communication such as electronic mail and SMS messaging can cause problems with personal relationships because of three main shortcomings with these media: their impersonal nature, their inability to capture tone and sarcasm and their easy accessibility at times of anger.

Conclusion:

While email and texts may therefore be useful for certain aspects of our daily lives, these communication methods need to be handled with care in some situations, particularly when they could be seen as insensitive, when it is possible that the recipient might misinterpret the meaning or when composed at times of personal agitation or stress. The writer of the message should use judgment and common sense in order to avoid the ill feelings that may be caused to the recipient in these cases.

Original wording in the introduction:	**Paraphrasing in the conclusion:**
email and SMS technologies have made our lives easier in a variety of ways	
there are certain drawbacks to emails and texts	
cannot capture the nuances	
subtleties of verbal communication	

Linking words and phrases in the conclusion:

What advice or prediction is made in the conclusion?

Writing the Conclusion – Answer

Original wording in the introduction:	Paraphrasing in the conclusion:
email and SMS technologies have made our lives easier in a variety of ways	email and texts may therefore be useful for certain aspects of our daily lives
there are certain drawbacks to emails and texts	these communication methods need to be handled with care in some situations
cannot capture the nuances	could be seen as insensitive . . .
subtleties of verbal communication	the recipient might misinterpret the meaning

Linking words and phrases in the conclusion:

while

particularly

when

in order to

What advice or prediction is made in the conclusion?

The following piece of advice is given in the last sentence of the conclusion to the essay: The writer of the message should use judgment and common sense in order to avoid the ill feelings that may be caused to the recipient in these cases.

Sample Task 2 Essay

We reproduce here in full our sample task 2 essay, which we have worked on throughout the previous sections of this study guide.

Sample Essay Task 2:

There is no disputing the fact that email and SMS technologies have made our lives easier in a variety of ways. Nevertheless, many of us will have had the experience of falling out with a friend or loved one over an email or text message whose content was poorly written or misconstrued. Clearly, there are certain drawbacks to emails and texts since electronic messaging cannot capture the nuances and subtleties of verbal communication. Modern forms of communication such as electronic mail and SMS messaging can cause problems with personal relationships because of three main shortcomings with these media: their impersonal nature, their inability to capture tone and sarcasm and their easy accessibility at times of anger.

Depending upon the context, the recipient of an email or text message may consider this mode of communication to be insensitive or uncaring. Although email may be practical for conveying straightforward information or facts, electronic messaging would be remarkably inappropriate for events like announcing a death. There is no direct human contact in emails and texts, and during times of loss or tragedy, human warmth and depth of emotion can only truly be conveyed through a phone call, or better still, by talking face to face.

A further problem with emails and texts is that they do not always accurately express the tone which the writer has intended. For instance, it might be possible for the recipient of a sarcastic email message to take its contents literally. The tone of the message may seem abundantly clear to the person who sent it, but sarcastic or ironically humorous utterances can only really be communicated in speech through the tone and inflection of the voice. Without the aid of tone and inflection, certain phrases in an email may come across as demanding, indifferent or rude.

The danger of having an accessible messaging service readily at hand during times of high emotion is another insidious problem with electronic media. In this day and age, we have heard stories not only of personal break ups that have been conducted by text, but also of employers who fire their staff by email message. Unless the writer of the message has the discipline and self-control to give him or herself a period of reasoned contemplation before sending the communication, he or she might send a regrettable message that can cause irretrievable damage to a relationship.

While email and texts may therefore be useful for certain aspects of our daily lives, these communication methods need to be handled with care in some situations, particularly when they could be seen as insensitive, when it is possible that the recipient might misinterpret the meaning or when composed at times of personal agitation or stress. The writer of the message should use judgment and common sense in order to avoid the ill feelings that may be caused to the recipient in these cases.

Now go to the writing practice tests on the next page and try writing responses to the tasks on your own.

PART 6 – IELTS WRITING PRACTICE TESTS

IELTS Writing Practice Test 1

TASK 1

You should spend about 20 minutes in this task.

The chart below shows infant mortality rates in three different countries from 1940 to 2010.

Summarise the information by selecting and reporting the main features and by making comparisons where appropriate.

Write at least 150 words.

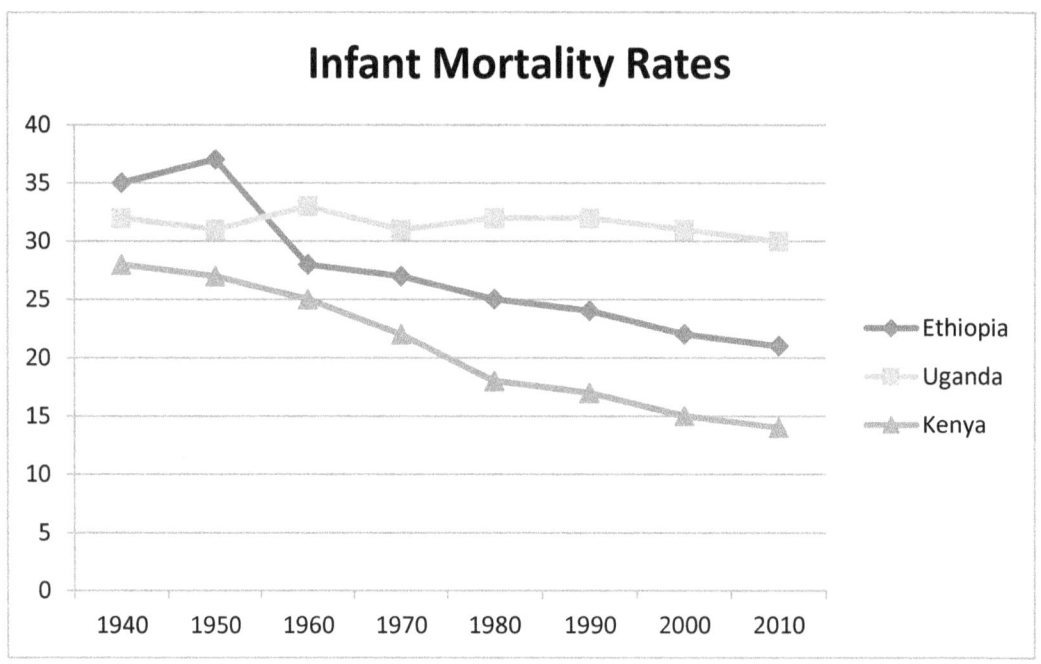

WRITING TASK 2

You should spend about 40 minutes in this task.

Television programs are of no value for children.

To what extent to you agree or disagree?

Provide explanations and examples to support your answer. You may draw on your own knowledge and experience.

Write at least 250 words.

Model Essays for Writing Practice Test 1

Practice Test 1, Writing Task 1

This model answer has been prepared as an example of a high-level answer. However, note that there are many possible ways to answer this type of question.

The graph shows infant death rates in Ethiopia, Uganda and Kenya for the period 1940 to 2010. The graph indicates that statistics on infant deaths in all three countries have generally improved over the past seven decades.

In 1940, the percentage of infant mortality was at its highest in all three countries at 35% in Ethiopia, 23% in Uganda and 27% in Kenya. However, the figures for Ethiopia and Kenya have fallen noticeably, while the infant mortality rate for Uganda dipped only slightly in 1950 and 1970.

In spite of some fluctuations in the percentages over the years, it appears that the amount of infants dying in the Ethiopian and Kenyan populations has fallen by approximately 13% in each country over the seventy-year period. On the other hand, the mortality rate for infants in Uganda has remained largely unchanged overall.

Practice Test 1, Writing Task 2

This model answer has been prepared as an example of a high-level answer. Comments on the essay are provided below.

Television programs are of no value for children.

To what extent to you agree or disagree?

Provide explanations and examples to support your answer. You may draw on your own knowledge and experience.

Televisual media h*as become* a **pervasive** force in the lives of families around the world today. Yet, a central question remains regarding whether watching television *is* harmful or **beneficial** for children. An analysis of this question *reveals* that television programs present three major concerns in the case of children, including depictions of violence, the use of **profane** language and the representation of poor moral role models.

Television programs that portray violence *are* a **paramount** concern for parents nowadays. Recent research has shown that children may commit acts of violence because they wish to **emulate** the behaviour that they *see* on television. This is especially true when violent acts *are committed* by well-known action "heroes". In addition, television programs *show* cartoon figures, as well as actors, committing violent acts. Using comic situations to depict violent themes *causes* further problems with the way in which young people view violence.

Television programs that *contain* profane or **disrespectful** language <u>also worry</u> parents with young children. <u>Because</u> **censorship** laws *have relaxed* over the past few decades, it *has become* very common for television programs of each and every kind to show characters expressing impolite, rude and insulting **utterances** to one another. Children unfortunately often *try* to **imitate** the actions they *watch* on their television screens, meaning that their behaviour sometimes <u>bears resemblance to</u> these portrayals of violence.

<u>Finally</u>, some parents *are* upset about the moral behaviour depicted on television. <u>As</u> they *struggle* to teach their children moral and **ethical** values, parents might *despair* about the lack of morals and ethics represented in some of the so-called role models on television. <u>For instance</u>, certain characters <u>not only</u> *have* no **remorse** for their immoral actions, <u>but also</u> frequently *go* unpunished by larger society.

<u>Because of these factors</u>, many parents *believe* that television programs *send* their youth the wrong kinds of messages. The **emulation** of this poor behaviour by their children *is* something they *wish* to avoid at all costs, and they *have* <u>accordingly</u> *decided* to **ban** television in their households <u>for these reasons</u>.

COMMENTS:

The essay above is high level for the following reasons:

1) It demonstrates excellent topic development. Each paragraph contains reasons and examples to support the student's point of view.

2) It is well organised. Pay attention to the underlined words and phrases, which the student uses to make the essay flow well.

3) The essay is grammatically correct. Notice that task 2 essays usually use verbs in the simple present or present perfect tenses. These tenses are needed because you will be asked to write about a topic of recent importance. You should therefore study the verb tenses in *italics*.

4) The essay contains high-level academic vocabulary. Please notice the words in **bold**. Try to learn these words if you don't know them already.

IELTS Writing Practice Test 2

TASK 1

You should spend about 20 minutes in this task.

The chart below shows the different degree subjects studied by male and female students at the University of the East of England. Summarise the information by selecting and reporting the main features and by making comparisons where appropriate.

Write at least 150 words.

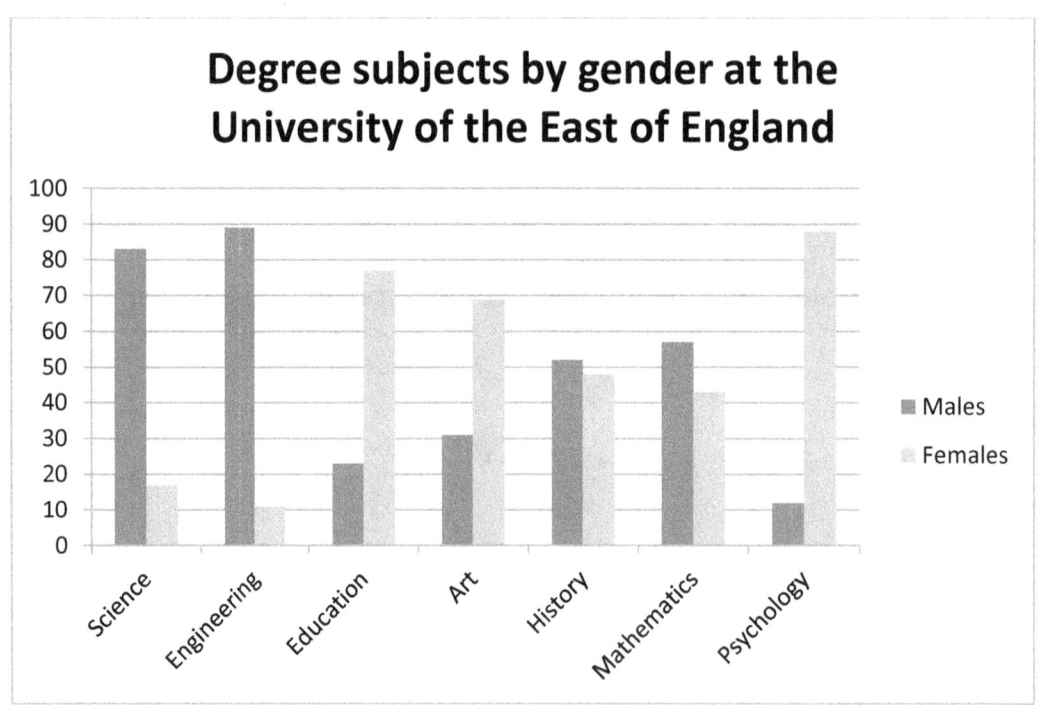

TASK 2

You should spend about 40 minutes in this task.

Advertising provides important information to consumers.

To what extent to you agree or disagree?

Provide explanations and examples to support your answer. You may draw on your own knowledge and experience.

Write at least 250 words.

Model Essays for Writing Practice Test 2

Practice Test 2, Writing Task 1

This model answer has been prepared as an example of a high-level answer. However, note that there are many possible ways to answer this type of question.

> The bar graph gives data about the subjects of degrees for men and women studying at the University of the East of England.
>
> One can readily discern that there are noticeable differences in the proportion of male and female students in various academic disciplines. The greatest gender difference is in the subject of engineering, which contains an 88% male enrolment, compared with only 12% for women in that subject. On the other hand, psychology was largely a female-dominated area, attracting a contingent of 87% women and only 13% men.
>
> The most equally balanced area of study in terms of the gender of its students was the subject of history, which had 52% male and 48% female students. This was closely followed by mathematics, whose subject statistics showed 57% men and 43% women.
>
> Overall, we can see that men appear to have a preference for scientific subjects, while women seem to prefer subjects in the humanities and social sciences.

Practice Test 2, Writing Task 2

This model answer has been prepared as an example of a high-level answer. Comments on the essay are provided below.

Advertising provides important information to consumers.

To what extent to you agree or disagree?

Provide explanations and examples to support your answer. You may draw on your own knowledge and experience.

Advertising is a pervasive force in today's market-driven economy. Consumers are bombarded with advertising at every turn, from advertisements on television and radio, to outdoor advertising on billboards and even on buses. This essay will demonstrate that advertising is essential for consumers since it provides information about products which would otherwise not be available and ensures the best prices to consumers through the perpetuation of competition and free enterprise.

First of all, advertisements give up-to-date information about products to consumers. If there were no advertising, consumers would not be *cognisant* of the benefits of certain products, but rather would be dependent upon word of mouth from their local shopkeepers, who may not be acting in the customer's best interests. Further, advertising helps to sell goods to a larger market. Therefore, as more goods are sold to the public, they become cheaper since they can be mass produced in order to meet demand.

On the other hand, some people may argue that advertisements do not truly give information to consumers, but rather persuade them merely to buy the products in question. This *phenomenon* creates a false economy, they argue, in which a demand is created for goods which are not really necessary. This argument also *contends* that children are particularly influenced by this false demand.

In conclusion, advertising is of *paramount* importance in today's market-driven economy because it not only informs the customer, but also helps to establish competitive prices. While some government *intervention* may be necessary to regulate advertising to children, most consumers are generally mature and intelligent enough to realise that while advertising presents information about a product, it will necessarily do so in the most flattering and *constructive* means possible. Indeed, the slogan 'Let the Buyer Beware', should be balanced against the freedom of choice afforded through advertising.

COMMENTS:

1) Again notice how each paragraph contains reasons and examples to support the student's point of view.

2) The essay contains a clear thesis statement at the end of the first paragraph.

3) The introduction and conclusion are clear and well-written.

4) The conclusion contains a feasible recommendation.

5) The main body is well organised. Notice the underlined words and phrases, which the student uses to make the essay flow well.

6) The essay is grammatically correct.

7) The essay contains very high-level academic vocabulary. Please notice the words in *italics*.

IELTS Writing Practice Test 3

TASK 1

You should spend about 20 minutes in this task.

The table below shows information on vehicle ownership by different types of households in the United Kingdom.

Summarise the information by selecting and reporting the main features and by making comparisons where appropriate.

Write at least 150 words.

Household type	Percentage of households of this type which own 2 or more vehicles (and total number of households)
single person	17% (59,000)
pre-retirement age couple, with no children	54% (234,000)
pre-retirement age couple with children	78% (378,000)
single parent with children	23% (117,000)
retired couple	4% (56,000)
All households	35% (844,000)

TASK 2

You should spend about 40 minutes in this task.

"The internet provides only useless information". Do you agree? Why or why not?

Provide explanations and examples to support your answer.

Write at least 250 words.

Model Essays for Writing Practice Test 3

Practice Test 3, Writing Task 1

This model answer has been prepared as an example of a high-level answer. However, note that there are many possible ways to answer this type of question.

> The table provides a breakdown of vehicle ownership for various types of households in the United Kingdom.
>
> On average, 35 percent of all families, consisting of nearly 844,000 households, owned two or more vehicles during this year. However, those households comprising couples with children had more than double this proportion, at 78% of the 378,000 households in this category.
>
> The lowest level of vehicle ownership was by the 56,000 households of retired couples, of which only 4% possessed more than one vehicle. The next lowest proportion was single person households, at 17% of the 59,000 households in this category.
>
> Conversely, households of pre-retirement age couples tend to own the greatest proportion of automobiles. In comparison to elderly couples, pre-retirement age couples own more automobiles perhaps because these households include people of driving age who use their automobiles for work.
>
> Generally, it is noticeable that households with more than one adult have the highest level of vehicle ownership. Nevertheless, elderly households are the exception to this general principle.

Practice Test 3, Writing Task 2

This model answer has been prepared as an example of a high-level answer. Comments on the essay are provided below.

"The internet provides only useless information". Do you agree? Why or why not? Provide explanations and examples to support your answer.

Many people believe that the internet is essential for communication in our modern society. On the other hand, there are those who hold the view that the internet contains worthless or *offensive* information. This essay will show that although the internet needs to be used cautiously in some circumstances, it also contains some helpful educational materials and factual data.

It is true that internet usage needs to be approached *vigilantly* on certain occasions. For example, parents with children often worry about them accessing websites that contain violent, illegal or sexual materials. This, in turn, could negatively influence children during the *formative* years of their personality development. In addition, so-called "information" on the internet needs to be read with a *critical* mind. Since anyone can set up a website, the qualifications of the site owner, as well as the accuracy and quality of the information on the site need to be *perused* sceptically.

In spite of these *caveats*, the internet is also practical for our daily lives. First of all, it makes some daily tasks more convenient. For instance, a person can now book airline tickets and make travel arrangements in the comfort of his or her living room with the click of a mouse. There are also websites that contain *indispensable* factual information. Consider the case of someone who wants to quit smoking. He or she can use any search engine to find webpages that offer help and advice with this situation. In addition, many of these types of websites are established by governmental agencies or charitable organisations, so the user can be confident that the information contained on these webpages is trustworthy.

To sum up, there are of course some situations in which users of the World Wide Web need to be *prudent*. Yet, there are also many helpful and accurate websites as well. It is up to each adult individual or parent, in the case of children, to decide which websites they are going to access.

COMMENTS:

1) This essay, like the previous sample essays, is well-organised and has correctly used advanced grammatical structures.

2) We provide underlined examples of more connective words and phrases, which the student uses to make the essay flow well.

3) You should again study the high-level academic vocabulary. Please review the words in *italics*. Try to learn these words if you don't know them already.

PART 7 – REVIEW OF VERB USAGE AND TENSE

Active voice:

Present simple tense

The present simple tense is used for habitual actions.

> Example: He goes to the office at 8:00 every morning.

The present tense is also used to state facts or generalisations.

> Example: Water freezes at zero degrees Celsius.

The present simple tense is formed as follows:

- I work.
- You work.
- He /She /It works.
- We work.
- You work. (Plural)
- They work.

Past simple tense

The past simple tense is used for actions that were started and completed in the past.

> Example: I walked three miles yesterday.

The past simple tense is formed as follows:

- I worked.

- You worked.
- He /She /It worked.
- We worked.
- You worked. (Plural)
- They worked.

Please note that the above example contains the regular verb "work". You should also be acquainted with the irregular verb forms for the exam.

Future simple tense

The future simple tense is used for actions that will occur in the future.

Example: Jane will study in the evening tomorrow.

The future simple tense is formed as follows:

- I will work.
- You will work.
- He /She /It will work.
- We will work.
- You will work. (Plural)
- They will work.

> **Simple tenses:**
> Present simple – habits, truths or generalisations
> Past simple – actions completed in the past
> Future simple – actions to be completed in the future

Present perfect tense

The present perfect tense is used for actions that were completed in the past, but that have relevancy in the present time.

Example: I have studied every day this week.

The phrase "this week" shows that the action has relevancy in the present time.

The present perfect tense is formed as follows:

- I have worked.
- You have worked.
- He /She /It has worked.
- We have worked.
- You have worked. (Plural)
- They have worked.

Past perfect tense

The past perfect is often used for an action which has just recently occurred.

The past perfect form can also be used to show that one action preceded another when a sentence describes two past actions. In this situation, the past perfect is used for the action which happened first. The simple past is used for the subsequent action.

The past perfect is often used with the words "just" and "after", and with the phrase "no sooner . . . than".

> Example: I had just finished writing her an email when she called me.

There are two actions in the above sentence, but the action of writing was finished before the action of calling.

The word "just" is often used with the past perfect tense, as in the example above.

REMEMBER: The auxiliary verb must come before the word "just".

> Example: When we had just arrived, she decided to leave.

"No sooner" is a negative adverbial. Accordingly, the auxiliary verb needs to be inverted in these sentences.

> Example: No sooner had we arrived, than she decided to leave.

The negative adverbial is an advanced grammatical skill. Accordingly, later in this section of the study guide, we provide a separate unit on using the past perfect with negative adverbials.

The past perfect tense is formed as follows:

- I had worked.
- You had worked.
- He /She /It had worked.

- We had worked.
- You had worked. (Plural)
- They had worked.

Future perfect tense

The future perfect tense is used to describe an action that will be completed at a definite time in the future.

> Example: By this time next week, I will have finished all of my exams.

The future perfect tense is formed as follows:

- I will have worked.
- You will have worked.
- He /She /It will have worked.
- We will have worked.
- You will have worked. (Plural)
- They will have worked.

> **Perfect tenses:**
> Present perfect – actions completed in the past, but relevant in the present time
> Past perfect – an action in the past that is relevant in the present and was completed before another action in the past.
> Future perfect – actions to be completed by a specific time in the future

Present simple progressive

The present simple progressive is used to describe actions that are in progress at the time of speaking.

> Example: He is studying for his final exams right now.

The present simple progressive is also used to describe actions that will take place at a fixed time in the future.

> Example: He is leaving for London on Tuesday.

The present simple progressive is formed as follows:

- I am working.
- You are working.
- He /She /It is working.
- We are working.
- You are working. (Plural)
- They are working.

Past simple progressive

The past simple progressive is used for actions that were in progress in the past.

The past simple progressive can be used to indicate that an action was in progress in the past when it was interrupted by a subsequent action.

Example: I was cleaning the house yesterday when the doorbell rang.

The past simple progressive is formed as follows:

- I was working.
- You were working.
- He /She /It was working.
- We were working.
- You were working. (Plural)
- They were working.

Future simple progressive

The future simple progressive is used for actions that will be in progress in the future.

Example: Jane will be travelling around the world next year.

The future simple tense is formed as follows:

- I will be working.
- You will be working.
- He /She /It will be working.
- We will be working.
- You will be working. (Plural)
- They will be working.

Present perfect progressive

The present perfect progressive is used for actions that were in progress in the past, but that have relevancy in the present time.

>Example: I have been working very hard lately.

The phrase "lately" shows that the action has relevancy in the present time.

The present perfect progressive is formed as follows:

- I have been working.
- You have been working.
- He /She /It has been working.
- We have been working.
- You have been working. (Plural)
- They have been working.

Progressive forms:
Present simple progressive – action is in progress at the time of speaking or is to take place at a definite time in the future
Past simple progressive – actions in progress in the past
Future simple progressive – actions to be in progress in the future

---

Passive voice:

Use the passive voice to emphasise the object of the action, rather than the person who was conducting the action.

In the example sentences that follow in this section, the diplomas are the object of the action.

We want to emphasise the fact that students are receiving the diplomas.

We want to de-emphasise the fact that the university officials are the people responsible for handing out the diplomas.

In other words, we could write the present simple passive example sentence below in the active voice, like this:

> Example: The university officials hand out diplomas on graduation day every year.

Present simple passive

The present simple passive is used in the sentence below because this form describes generalisations or things that normally occur in a predictable way.

> Example: Diplomas are handed out on graduation day every year.

Past simple passive

The past simple passive is used in the sentence below because it describes the object of an action that was completed in the past.

> Example: Diplomas were handed out on graduation day last year.

Future simple passive

The future simple passive is used in the sentence below because it describes the object of an action that will be completed in the future.

> Example: Diplomas will be handed out on graduation day in May this year.

Future passive with is/are

The "future passive with is/are" form is used in the sentence below because it describes an action that is planned for the future.

> Example: Diplomas are to be handed out on graduation day in May this year.

Present simple progressive passive

The present progressive passive is used in the sentence below because we are talking about an action that will take place during a definite time in the future. This form emphasises that a plan is in place for the event.

> Example: Diplomas are being handed out on graduation day, which is May 18th this year.

Past simple progressive passive

The past simple progressive passive is used in the sentence below because this action was in progress in the past, and we want to put an emphasis on the object of that action.

Example: The diplomas were being handed out on graduation day when the ceremony was interrupted.

Present perfect passive

The present perfect passive is used in the sentence below because it emphasises that the diplomas have been handed out like this in the past, and that this action continues in the present.

Example: Diplomas have been handed out on graduation day since the university was founded in 1924.

Past perfect passive

The past perfect passive is used in the sentence below because it emphasises that the diplomas were handed out like this in the past, but the policy on handing out diplomas in this way has recently changed.

Example: Diplomas had been handed out on graduation day until last year, when they started to be sent in the mail.

Passive form:
Remember to use one of the passive forms to emphasise the object of the action, rather than the action itself.

Gerunds and Infinitives:

A gerund is a verbal noun which ends in "ing", while the infinitive consists of "to" and the base form of the verb.

Some verbs always take an infinitive (to + verb) and some always take a gerund (the –ing form). However, some will take either.

Look at the following examples and study the lists that follow.

INFINITIVE:

    CORRECT: Sarah decided to go out.

    INCORRECT: Sarah decided going out.

Here are some more examples of the infinitive:

He agreed to pay half the cost.

She refused to wait.

The man had chosen not to buy a ticket.

GERUND:

    CORRECT: Sarah suggested going out.

    INCORRECT: Sarah suggested to go out.

Here are some more examples of the gerund:

He recommended paying half the cost.

I practice playing the piano.

She admitted not buying a ticket.

These verbs and phrases take the infinitive:

advise

agree

aim

appear

arrange

ask

attempt

be just about (ready)

beg

can't afford

can't wait

choose

claim

decide

demand

enable

expect

fail

guarantee

happen

hesitate

hope

it's time

learn

long

manage

mean

neglect

offer

omit

pay

plan

prepare

pretend

promise

prove

refuse

seem

swear

tend

there's no reason

threaten

turn out

want

wish

These verbs and phrases take the gerund:

admit

appreciate

avoid

be in the habit of

be tired of

can't help

can't stand

confess

consider

contemplate

delay

deny

detest

dislike

don't mind

enjoy

escape

excuse

finish

give up

have trouble

How about . . .?

imagine

involve

justify

keep

keep on

mention

miss

not be worth

postpone

practice

put off

quit

recommend

resent

resist

risk

save

suggest

thinking about

thought of

tolerate

These verbs can take either the infinitive or the gerund: start, continue, intend, like and hate.

For example, both of these sentences as are correct:

> Andrew started to unpack his suitcase.
>
> Andrew started unpacking his suitcase.

Finally, remember that gerunds are usually used to speak about hobbies.

> I enjoy swimming.
>
> He can't stand hiking.

You will see a separate unit on gerunds and infinitives, with further examples and exercises, later in this section of the study guide.

Modal verbs:

You may see questions on the grammar/usage test on modal verbs.

Modal verbs are used to express obligation, certainty, possibility or permission.

Most commonly, the test assesses the modal verbs "should", "would" and "can".

However, sometimes other modal verbs such as "could", "may", "might" and "must" are also included on the exam.

can:

The modal verb "can" is used to show permission or possibility.

A general possibility: Learning a language can be difficult.

Permission: I can drive her car when she is out of town.

The word "can" is also used in passive sentence constructions, like in the examples below.

> Example – Active voice: You can declare that income on your tax return.
>
> Example – Passive voice: That income can be declared on your tax return.

could:

The modal verb "could" is used to make suggestions and polite requests, as well as to talk about past possibilities and future possibilities.

Suggestion: You could spend your holiday in Thailand.

Polite request: Could I read that book when you have finished it?

Past possibility: I could have failed the examination. I certainly hadn't studied enough for it.

Future possibility: He could be found guilty of the crime when the police have finished their investigation.

may:

The modal verb "may" is used to talk about present or future possibilities or to give permission.

Present possibility: She may be upset right now, so I wouldn't tell her more bad news.

Future possibility: She may be upset if you decide to lie to her.

Permission: You may leave the table when you have finished eating.

might:

The modal verb "might" is used to talk about future possibilities. It can also be used to talk about past possibilities.

Future possibility: She might take a taxi home since the party is going to finish late.

Past possibility: I might have failed the driving test. I certainly didn't feel prepared.

must:

The modal verb "must" is used to express certainty or necessity.

Certainty: That must have been the restaurant. It's the only one on the street.

Necessity (for something that is necessary): You must have a valid library card to check out a book.

should:

The word "should" is used to give advice or to express expectation or obligation. "Should" needs to be used with another verb.

Advice: You should study hard for your exam.

Expectation: You should be able to finish the work within three days.

Obligation: You should have returned the video on time. Now you will have to pay a late fee.

would:

The modal verb "would" can be used to express one's thoughts on an action in the past. Be sure to avoid the "would of" construction, which is not grammatical.

>CORRECT: I would have studied more if I had known the exam was going to be so difficult.

>INCORRECT: I would of studied more if I had known the exam was going to be so difficult.

The correct sentence above containing "would" is an example of the third conditional sentence structure.

You will see separate units on modal verbs and the third conditional, with further examples and exercises, later in this section of the study guide.

Phrasal verbs and prepositions:

Many students struggle with phrasal verbs and prepositions. Indeed, even advanced-level learners of English can have difficulties with these skills.

Unlike verb tense and form, phrasal verbs and prepositions cannot be classified into categories of usage according to situations or time.

In other words, phrasal verbs and prepositions cannot really be explained. They are something that simply needs to be learned from memory.

So, for phrasal verbs, you will need to learn each verb and its stem, as well as its meaning, by studying and memorising them.

Likewise, you will need to remember that certain nouns, verbs and adjectives are used with only one particular preposition.

You will see separate units on phrasal verbs and prepositions, with further examples and exercises, later in this section of the study guide.

PART 8 – ADDITIONAL GRAMMAR EXERCISES

Gerunds and Infinitives – Exercises

Exercise: Complete the following sentences by using either the gerund or infinitive form of the verb provided.

1) It's not worth (write) the whole letter over again.

2) Gunther refused (listen) to what we had to say.

3) He denied (steal) the stereo.

4) Martina is in the habit of (stay up) quite late.

5) I advise you (study) more.

6) He was just about (leave) when the telephone rang.

7) I apologise. I meant (tell) you about the party last week.

8) How about (go) to the cinema tonight?

9) I always have trouble (tie) this necktie.

10) As your manager, my job is checking (see) that you carry out your responsibilities.

11) The pianist is paid (play) music for the customers.

12) I have been thinking about (visit) my grandma next week.

13) She really enjoys (swim) in the summer.

14) It's time (pack) our things and head home.

15) There's no reason (cry) about it.

16) I'm really tired of (hear) him complain all the time.

17) Have you ever considered (cut) your hair short?

18) I hope (win) the lottery and live in Brazil someday.

19) Imagine (have) a million pounds!

20) You must be prepared (study) a lot if you want to succeed at university.

Modal Verbs – Exercises

Exercise: Complete the following sentences, placing a modal verb in the space provided. Some sentences may have more than one answer. The number of gaps in each sentence indicates the number of possible answers.

1) You _____ have told us you weren't coming. We waited for over an hour. OBLIGATION

2) There are several ways to get to Norwich from here. You _____ even take the train. SUGGESTION

3) Paloma said she _____ / _____ / _____ be going to the picnic tomorrow. She wasn't sure. FUTURE POSSIBILITY

4) You have a terrible cough. You _____ go to the doctor. ADVICE

5) He _____ have gone out for the night. He's not answering the phone. CERTAINTY

6) _____ / _____ / _____ I have another slice of cake, please? PERMISSION (2) / POLITE REQUEST (1)

7) The weather forecast said it _____ / _____ / _____ rain tomorrow. FUTURE POSSIBILITY

8) A good mother _____ / _____ always be concerned with the welfare of her children. NECESSITY (1) / ADVICE (1)

9) All taxpayers _____ register with Revenue and Customers when they have an income – it's the law. NECESSITY

10) What an awful accident. We _____ / _____ have been killed. PAST POSSIBILITY

Past Perfect – Exercises

Exercise: Change the verbs given in the following sentences, using the past perfect and the past simple tense in each sentence. Note that many of the sentences use the negative adverbial structure.

1) No sooner _____ (we get) on the motorway than our car _____ (break down).

2) No sooner _____ (I finish) speaking on the phone than the doorbell _____ (ring).

3) Someone _____ (tell) Bethany before I _____ (have) a chance.

4) Carlos _____ (tear up) that note before I _____ (see) it.

5) I _____ (see) the wedding dress you _____ (choose).

6) She _____ (receive) the letter several days after I _____ (mail) it.

7) No sooner _____ (the fire start) than the alarm _____ (go off).

8) After Lamar _____ (become) sleepy, he _____ (leave) the party.

9) Just when the party _____ (begin), we _____ (see) Fang come in the door.

10) I _____ (just say) goodbye to Suki when Bao Yu _____ (arrive).

Phrasal Verbs – Exercises

The following exercises will help you review phrasal verb usage.

Exercise: Match the phrasal verb on the left to the correct meaning provided on the right.

PART A

1.	She just <u>barged into</u> the room without knocking.	A.	to make more talkative
2.	We all <u>chipped in</u> to buy Aisha a birthday present.	B.	to convert
3.	He is really very shy, but if you talk to him, you can <u>draw</u> him <u>out</u>.	C.	to enter without knocking
4.	They are going to <u>knock down</u> the old cinema next week.	D.	to endure
5.	They are <u>turning</u> their garage <u>into</u> an extra bedroom.	E.	to admire
6.	Do you know where I can <u>get a hold of</u> yesterday's newspaper?	F.	to acquire

7. The college's fee increase nearly brought about a protest.

G. to contribute

8. Running that marathon really did me in.

H. to cause exhaustion

9. I really look up to you for your courage.

I. to make a mistake

10. I can ignore your error this time but don't slip up again.

J. to demolish

PART B

1. Raquel is far from taciturn. In fact, she can really <u>ramble on</u>.
2. None of the students knew what the professor was <u>driving at</u>.
3. Being successful in business <u>calls for</u> insight and hard work.
4. You <u>bring on</u> most of your problems by yourself.
5. Newspaper reporters are always trying to <u>dig up</u> gossip.
6. That really annoys me. I wish you would <u>cut it out</u>.
7. If you don't stop working so hard you will <u>run</u> yourself <u>down</u>.
8. Smoking outside the hospital entrance is <u>frowned on</u>.

A. to require or necessitate
B. to locate with difficulty
C. to create poor health
D. to cease
E. to cause
F. to disapprove of something
G. to revoke
H. to talk incessantly

9. I thought that I wasn't going to like the party, but it <u>turned out</u> to be fun.

I. to occur or happen

10. I hope you won't <u>go back on</u> your promise to help me.

J. to mean something

PART C

1. Enrique <u>bailed out of</u> the agreement after having second thoughts.
2. The football match was <u>called off</u> due to the rain.
3. Why do you <u>keep on</u> doing that? I've told you a million times to stop.
4. Julia didn't <u>let on</u> that she knew about the surprise party.
5. I had to wait at the town hall while they <u>brought up</u> my information on the computer.
6. Dave is such a bully. He should <u>pick on</u> somebody his own size for a change.
7. You can <u>pick out</u> any of the tomatoes you like, madam.

A. to withdraw from
B. to locate something
C. to choose
D. to audition for or test
E. to betray a secret
F. to provide transport
G. to persist

8. Be ready at 8:00 sharp. I'll <u>pick</u> you <u>up</u> at the front door.

9. Sarah is going to <u>try out</u> for the choir next week.

10. You shouldn't <u>take on</u> more responsibilities than you can handle.

H. to tease or torment

I. to accept

J. to cancel

Prepositions – Exercises

The following exercises will help you review your preposition usage.

Exercise: Place appropriate prepositions in the spaces provided.

1) After 25 years _____ marriage, she is still faithful _____ her husband and devoted _____ her children.

2) It took him several months to recover _____ his viral infection.

3) The politician was completely devoid _____ integrity.

4) The subject of building a new hotel is currently _____ discussion.

5) I was given a writing set for my birthday, consisting _____ paper and pens.

6) She was really pleased _____ receiving first prize.

7) The success of any business is contingent _____ the strength of its management.

8) John hadn't expected such an icy reception. In fact, he was really taken _____ surprise.

9) You will never be healthy is your diet is deficient _____ vitamins.

10) Police officers are _____ duty all day long.

11) Could you give me a little help _____ my chemistry assignment?

12) She had gained so much weight that she was really ashamed _____ herself.

13) The manager will investigate the matter and will contact you _____ writing.

14) It was love at first sight. She fell _____ him the moment they first met.

15) That author is famous _____ his horror stories.

16) It has taken me a long time to get accustomed _____ living in this area.

17) She really loves her car and would hate to part _____ it.

18) Many species are threatened _____ extinction nowadays.

19) If you refuse to work hard, your endeavours will amount _____ nothing.

20) I hope you're going to stand _____ your promise.

21) Jamila is really pleased _____ Amir for being so cooperative.

22) Ali really likes listening _____ music in his free time.

23) Many homes are not insured _____ earthquake damage.

24) Will you exchange your old car _____ a different model?

25) His version of the story was not consistent _____ the facts.

26) You will be given a refund in accordance _____ the terms _____ the product warranty.

27) Six out _____ ten residents of this city have attended university.

28) I don't approve _____ your behaviour.

29) I haven't been introduced _____ him, although I know him _____ sight.

30) Robert's company has always operated _____ a profit.

Third Conditional – Exercises

The third conditional is used to hypothesise, or make a guess about, how a past event could have happened differently. The following structure is used:

If + past perfect . . . would + have + past participle

The past perfect structure can also be inverted. Inversion involves removing the word "if" from the original sentence and beginning the new sentence with the word "had". The inverted sentence structure is often tested on the exam.

Look at this example:

Had she not been so careless, the fire would not have started.

This sentence has been inverted. It could be re-written as follows:

If she had not been so careless, the fire would not have started.

Exercise: Write one sentence for each of the following groups of sentences, using the inverted third conditional structure. You may need to add or remove the word "not" from either clause of the sentence you make.

1) Marek didn't drive carefully. He had an accident.

   Had Marek . . .

2) Pavel decided not to buy the car. She didn't like it.

Had Pavel . . .

3) I didn't pass my exam. I didn't study for it.

Had I . . .

4) Dasha didn't wear a sweater. She caught a cold.

Had Dasha . . .

5) I didn't prepare anything to eat. I didn't know you were coming.

Had I . . .

6) Zahra was so bored by the TV programme. She fell asleep.

Had Zahra . . .

7) The movie wasn't interesting. I left half-way through.

Had the movie . . .

8) I told my friend he was stupid. He left in a rage.

Had I not . . .

9) He argued with his boss. As a result, he was fired.

Had he not . . .

10) It rained all night. The football match was cancelled.

Had it not . . .

Grammar Exercises – Answers

Gerunds and Infinitives - Answers

1) writing

2) to listen

3) stealing

4) staying up

5) to study

6) to leave

7) to tell

8) going

9) tying

10) to see

11) to play

12) visiting

13) swimming

14) to pack

15) to cry

16) hearing

17) cutting

18) to win

19) having

20) to study

Modal Verbs - Answers

1) should

2) could

3) could, may, might

4) should

5) must

6) may, might, could

7) may, might, could

8) must, should

9) must

10) could, might

Past Perfect – Answers

1) No sooner had we gotten on the motorway than our car broke down.

2) No sooner had I finished speaking on the telephone than the doorbell rang.

3) Someone had told Bethany before I had a chance to.

4) Carlos had torn up that note before I saw it.

5) I saw the wedding dress you had chosen.

6) She received the letter several days after I had mailed it.

7) No sooner had the fire started than the alarm went off.

8) After Lamar had become sleepy, he left the party.

9) Just when the party had begun, we saw Nancy come in the door.

10) I had just said goodbye to Suki when Bao Yu arrived.

Phrasal Verbs – Answers

PART A

1) C

2) G

3) A

4) J

5) B

6) F

7) D

8) H

9) E

10) I

PART B

1) H

2) J

3) A

4) E

5) B

6) D

7) C

8) F

9) I

10) G

PART C

1) A

2) J

3) G

4) E

5) B

6) H

7) C

8) F

9) D

10) I

Prepositions – Answers

1) of, to, to

2) from

3) of

4) under

5) of

6) about

7) upon or on

8) by

9) in

10) on

11) with

12) of

13) in

14) for

15) for

16) to

17) with

18) with

19) to

20) by

21) with

22) to

23) for

24) for

25) with

26) with, of

27) of

28) of

29) to, by

30) at

The Third Conditional – Answers

1) Had Marek driven more carefully, he wouldn't have had an accident.

2) Had Pavel liked the car, she would have bought it.

3) Had I studied for my exam, I would have passed it.

4) Had Dasha worn a sweater, she wouldn't have caught a cold.

5) Had I known you were coming, I would have prepared something to eat.

6) Had Zahra not been so bored by the TV programme, she wouldn't have fallen asleep.

7) Had the movie been interesting, I wouldn't have left half-way through.

8) Had I not told my friend he was stupid, he wouldn't have left in a rage.

9) Had he not argued with his boss, he wouldn't have been fired.

10) Had it not rained all night, the football match wouldn't have been cancelled.

ESSAY CORRECTION EXERCISES

ESSAY CORRECTION EXERCISE 1

The draft essays that follow contain errors. Choose the correct version of each part of each sentence from the answer choices provided. If the part of the sentence is correct as written, you should choose answer A. The answers are provided at the end of the exercises.

[1] Antarctica is a mysterious and remote continent [2] one which is often forgotten by virtue of its geographical location. [3] Now that the Antarctic is remote and desolate. [4] Nevertheless, an understanding of the organisms that inhabit this continent was critical [5] to our comprehension of the world as a global community. [6] For this reason, the southernmost continent has the source of a great deal of scientific investigation.

[7] Many notable recent research has come from America and Great Britain. [8] The British Antarctic Survey, sponsored with the Natural Environment Research Council of the United Kingdom, [9] and the United States Antarctic Resource Center, a collaborate of the United States Geological Survey Mapping Division and the National Science Foundation, [10] are forerunners in the burgeoning currently field of research in this area.

[11] This corpus of research has resulted in an abundance of factual data on the Antarctic. [12] For example, one now know that more than ninety nine percent of the land is completely covered by snow and ice, [13] which making Antarctica the coldest continent on the planet. [14] This inhospitable climate, has not surprisingly, brought about the adaptation [15] of a plethora of plants and biological organisms on the continent present. [16] An investigation for the sedimentary geological formations

provides testimony to the process of adaptation. [17] Ancient sediment's recovered from the bottom of Antarctic lakes, [18] bacteria as well as discovered in ice, [19] has reveal the history of climate change over the past 10,000 years.

Item 1.
   A.   Antarctica is a mysterious and remote continent
   B.   Antarctica is a mysterious and resounding continent
   C.   Antarctica is a mysterious and respectable continent
   D.   Antarctica is a mysterious and resistant continent
   E.   Antarctica is a mysterious and restrained continent

Item 2.
   A.   one which is often forgotten by virtue of its geographical location.
   B.   one whose often forgotten by virtue of its geographical location.
   C.   that is often forgotten by virtue of its geographical location.
   D.   this is often forgotten by virtue of its geographical location.
   E.   those are often forgotten by virtue of its geographical location.

Item 3.
   A.   Now that the Antarctic is remote and desolate.
   B.   Always, the Antarctic is remote and desolate.
   C.   Since the Antarctic is remote and desolate.
   D.   Indeed, the Antarctic is remote and desolate.
   E.   On the other hand, the Antarctic is remote and desolate.

Item 4.
   A.   Nevertheless, an understanding of the organisms that inhabit this continent was critical
   B.   Nevertheless, an understanding of the organisms that inhabit this continent were critical
   C.   Nevertheless, an understanding of the organisms that inhabit this continent is critical
   D.   Nevertheless, an understanding of the organisms that inhabit this continent are critical
   E.   Nevertheless, an understanding of the organisms that inhabit this continent are being critical

Item 5.
- A. to our comprehension of the world as a global community.
- B. to our comprehension at the world as a global community.
- C. to our comprehension in the world as a global community.
- D. to our comprehension about the world as a global community.
- E. to our comprehension for the world as a global community.

Item 6.
- A. For this reason, the southernmost continent has the source of a great deal of scientific investigation.
- B. For this reason, the southernmost continent has been the source of a great deal of scientific investigation.
- C. For this reason, the southernmost continent was the source of a great deal of scientific investigation.
- D. For this reason, the southernmost continent has to be the source of a great deal of scientific investigation.
- E. For this reason, the southernmost continent had the source of a great deal of scientific investigation.

Item 7.
- A. Many notable recent research has come from America and Great Britain.
- B. Much notable recent research has come from America and Great Britain.
- C. More notable recent research has come from America and Great Britain.
- D. More than notable recent research has come from America and Great Britain.
- E. As much as notable recent research has come from America and Great Britain.

Item 8.
- A. The British Antarctic Survey, sponsored with the Natural Environment Research Council of the United Kingdom,
- B. The British Antarctic Survey, sponsored by the Natural Environment Research Council of the United Kingdom,
- C. The British Antarctic Survey, sponsored against the Natural Environment Research Council of the United Kingdom,

- D. The British Antarctic Survey, sponsored from the Natural Environment Research Council of the United Kingdom,
- E. The British Antarctic Survey, sponsored upon the Natural Environment Research Council of the United Kingdom,

Item 9.
- A. and the United States Antarctic Resource Center, a collaborate of the United States Geological Survey Mapping Division and the National Science Foundation,
- B. And the United States Antarctic Resource Center, a collaborative of the United States Geological Survey Mapping Division and the National Science Foundation,
- C. and the United States Antarctic Resource Center, a collaboratively of the United States Geological Survey Mapping Division and the National Science Foundation,
- D. and the United States Antarctic Resource Center, a collaboration of the United States Geological Survey Mapping Division and the National Science Foundation,
- E. and the United States Antarctic Resource Center, a collaborator of the United States Geological Survey Mapping Division and the National Science Foundation,

Item 10.
- A. are forerunners in the burgeoning currently field of research in this area.
- B. are forerunners in the burgeoning field of currently research in this area.
- C. are currently forerunners in the burgeoning field of research in this area.
- D. are forerunners in the burgeoning field of research in currently this area.
- E. are forerunners in the burgeoning field of research in this currently area.

Item 11.
- A. This corpus of research has resulted in an abundance of factual data on the Antarctic.
- B. This corpus of research was resulted in an abundance of factual data on the Antarctic.

C. This corpus of research has been resulted in an abundance of factual data on the Antarctic.
D. This corpus of research was resulting in an abundance of factual data on the Antarctic.
E. This corpus of research resulting in an abundance of factual data on the Antarctic.

Item 12.
A. For example, one now know that more than ninety nine percent of the land is completely covered by snow and ice,
B. For example, we now know that more than ninety nine percent of the land is completely covered by snow and ice,
C. For example, they now knows that more than ninety nine percent of the land is completely covered by snow and ice,
D. For example, the community now know that more than ninety nine percent of the land is completely covered by snow and ice,
E. For example, the research now know that more than ninety nine percent of the land is completely covered by snow and ice,

Item 13.
A. which making Antarctica the coldest continent on the planet.
B. which is making Antarctica the coldest continent on the planet.
C. making Antarctica the coldest continent on the planet.
D. has made Antarctica the coldest continent on the planet.
E. that made Antarctica the coldest continent on the planet.

Item 14.
A. This inhospitable climate, has not surprisingly, brought about the adaptation
B. This inhospitable climate has, not surprisingly, brought about the adaptation
C. This inhospitable climate has, not surprisingly; brought about the adaptation
D. This inhospitable climate has not surprisingly: brought about the adaptation
E. This inhospitable climate has not surprisingly, brought about the adaptation

Item 15.
- A. of a plethora of plants and biological organisms on the continent present.
- B. of a plethora of plants and biological organisms present on the continent.
- C. of a plethora on the continent of plants and biological organisms present.
- D. of a plethora of plants on the continent and biological organisms present.
- E. of a plethora of plants and on the continent biological organisms present.

Item 16.
- A. An investigation for the sedimentary geological formations provides testimony to the process of adaptation.
- B. An investigation within the sedimentary geological formations provides testimony to the process of adaptation.
- C. An investigation at the sedimentary geological formations provides testimony to the process of adaptation.
- D. An investigation about the sedimentary geological formations provides testimony to the process of adaptation.
- E. An investigation into the sedimentary geological formations provides testimony to the process of adaptation.

Item 17.
- A. Ancient sediment's recovered from the bottom of Antarctic lakes,
- B. Ancient sediments' recovered from the bottom of Antarctic lakes,
- C. Ancient sediments recovered from the bottom of Antarctic lakes,
- D. Ancient's sediment recovered from the bottom of Antarctic lakes,
- E. Ancient's sediments recovered from the bottom of Antarctic lakes,

Item 18.
- A. bacteria as well as discovered in ice,
- B. as well as bacteria discovered in ice,
- C. bacteria discovered as well as in ice,

D. bacteria discovered in as well as ice,
E. bacteria discovered in ice as well,

Item 19.
A. has reveal the history of climate change over the past 10,000 years.
B. has revealed the history of climate change over the past 10,000 years.
C. have reveal the history of climate change over the past 10,000 years.
D. have revealed the history of climate change over the past 10,000 years.
E. have been revealed the history of climate change over the past 10,000 years.

Item 20.
If the student were to add a paragraph at the end of the essay explaining that the reliability of the research on Antarctica has been disputed, the essay would lose:
A. its academic tone.
B. its clarity and focus.
C. the sense that this topic of current interest.
D. its emphasis on the inhospitality of the Antarctic climate.
E. the sense of importance it places on the scientific evidence.

ESSAY CORRECTION EXERCISE 2

[1] The major significant characteristic of any population is its age-sex structure, [2] defining as the proportion of people of each gender in each different age group. [3] The age-sex structure determines the potential for reproduction, [4] and for example population growth, [5] based on the balance of males and females of child-bearing age inside a population. [6] Thus, the age-sex structure was social policy implications.

[7] For instance, a population with a high proportion of citizens elderly [8] needs to consider its governmental-funded pension schemes and health care systems carefully. [9] As follows: a demographic with a greater

percentage of young children should ensure [10] which its educational funding and child welfare policies are implemented efficaciously.

[11] Accordingly, as the composition of a population changes against time, [12] the government may need to restate its funding priorities.

[13] For it is possible that a population may have low birth rates [14] resulting an imbalance in the age-sex structure. [15] Low birth rate's might also be attributable to governmental policy that attempts to control the population. [16] Policies are one example of that restrict the number of children a family can have this outcome.

[17] Other possible reason for these types of demographic changes might be unnaturally high death rates, [18] such like in the case of a disease epidemic or natural disaster. [19] Finally, migration is another factor [20] in demographic attrition, because in any population, a certain amount of people, may decide to emigrate, or move to a different country.

Item 1.
- A. The major significant characteristic of any population is its age-sex structure,
- B. The majorly significant characteristic of any population is its age-sex structure,
- C. The most significantly characteristic of any population is its age-sex structure,
- D. The most significant characteristic of any population is its age-sex structure,
- E. The more significant characteristic of any population is its age-sex structure,

Item 2.
- A. defining as the proportion of people of each gender in each different age group.
- B. defined as the proportion of people of each gender in each different age group.

- C. which defining as the proportion of people of each gender in each different age group.
  - D. which defined as the proportion of people of each gender in each different age group.
  - E. as defined as the proportion of people of each gender in each different age group.

Item 3.
  - A. The age-sex structure determines the potential for reproduction,
  - B. The age-sex structure determined the potential for reproduction,
  - C. The age-sex structure has determined the potential for reproduction,
  - D. The age-sex structure had determined the potential for reproduction,
  - E. The age-sex structure was determined the potential for reproduction,

Item 4.
  - A. and for example population growth,
  - B. and so that population growth,
  - C. and with regard to population growth,
  - D. and it follows that population growth,
  - E. and as a consequence population growth,

Item 5.
  - A. based on the balance of males and females of child-bearing age inside a population.
  - B. based on the balance of males and females of child-bearing age within a population.
  - C. based on the balance of males and females of child-bearing age containing a population.
  - D. based on the balance of males and females of child-bearing age consisting a population.
  - E. based on the balance of males and females of child-bearing age attributing a population.

Item 6.
  - A. Thus, the age-sex structure was social policy implications.
  - B. Thus, the age-sex structure is social policy implications.
  - C. Thus, the age-sex structure has social policy implications.

- D. Thus, the age-sex structure had social policy implications.
- E. Thus, the age-sex structure does social policy implications.

Item 7.
- A. For instance, a population with a high proportion of citizens elderly
- B. For instance, a population with an elderly high proportion of citizens
- C. For instance, a population with a high proportion elderly of citizens
- D. For instance, a population with a high proportion of elderly citizens
- E. For instance, a population with a high elderly proportion of citizens

Item 8.
- A. needs to consider its governmental-funded pension schemes and health care systems carefully.
- B. needs to consider its governmentally-funded pension schemes and health care systems carefully.
- C. needs to consider its funded-governmental pension schemes and health care systems carefully.
- D. needs to consider its funded-governmentally pension schemes and health care systems carefully.
- E. needs to consider its funded governmentally-pension schemes and health care systems carefully.

Item 9.
- A. As follows: a demographic with a greater percentage of young children should ensure
- B. Just as a demographic with a greater percentage of young children should ensure
- C. Conversely, a demographic with a greater percentage of young children should ensure
- D. Despite, a demographic with a greater percentage of young children should ensure
- E. Unless a demographic with a greater percentage of young children should ensure

Item 10.
- A. which its educational funding and child welfare policies are implemented efficaciously.
- B. that its educational funding and child welfare policies are implemented efficaciously.
- C. which it's educational funding and child welfare policies are implemented efficaciously.
- D. that it's educational funding and child welfare policies are implemented efficaciously.
- E. hence its educational funding and child welfare policies are implemented efficaciously.

Item 11.
- A. Accordingly, as the composition of a population changes against time,
- B. Accordingly, as the composition of a population changes for time,
- C. Accordingly, as the composition of a population changes over time,
- D. Accordingly, as the composition of a population changes past time,
- E. Accordingly, as the composition of a population changes as time,

Item 12.
- A. the government may need to restate its funding priorities.
- B. the government may need to re-evaluate its funding priorities.
- C. the government may need to recuperate its funding priorities.
- D. the government may need to cooperate its funding priorities.
- E. the government may need to instigate its funding priorities.

Item 13.
- A. For it is possible that a population may have low birth rates
- B. For this possible that a population may have low birth rates
- C. This is possible that a population may have low birth rates
- D. It is possible that a population may have low birth rates
- E. That is possible that a population may have low birth rates

Item 14.
- A. resulting an imbalance in the age-sex structure.
- B. because an imbalance in the age-sex structure.
- C. due to an imbalance in the age-sex structure.
- D. since an imbalance in the age-sex structure.
- E. in order to imbalance in the age-sex structure.

Item 15.
- A. Low birth rate's might also be attributable to governmental policy that attempts to control the population.
- B. Low birth's rates might also be attributable to governmental policy that attempts to control the population.
- C. Low births' rates might also be attributable to governmental policy that attempts to control the population.
- D. Low birth rates' might also be attributable to governmental policy that attempts to control the population.
- E. Low birth rates might also be attributable to governmental policy that attempts to control the population.

Item 16.
- A. Policies are one example of that restrict the number of children a family can have this outcome.
- B. Policies that restrict are one example of the number of children a family can have this outcome.
- C. Policies that restrict the number of children a family can have this outcome are one example.
- D. Policies that restrict the number of children a family can have are one example of this outcome.
- E. Policies that restrict the number of children a family are one example of this outcome can have.

Item 17.
- A. Other possible reason for these types of demographic changes might be unnaturally high death rates,
- B. Others possible reason for these types of demographic changes might be unnaturally high death rates,
- C. Another possible reason for these types of demographic changes might be unnaturally high death rates,
- D. Anothers possible reason for these types of demographic changes might be unnaturally high death rates,
- E. Another possible reasons for these types of demographic changes might be unnaturally high death rates,

Item 18.
- A. such like in the case of a disease epidemic or natural disaster.
- B. such as in the case of a disease epidemic or natural disaster.
- C. as such as in the case of a disease epidemic or natural disaster.
- D. as its in the case of a disease epidemic or natural disaster.
- E. as much like as in the case of a disease epidemic or natural disaster.

Item 19.
- A. Finally, migration is another factor
- B. Final migration is another factor
- C. Final, migration is another factor
- D. To end, migration is another factor
- E. Conclusively, migration is another factor

Item 20.
- A. in demographic attrition, because in any population, a certain amount of people, may decide to emigrate, or move to a different country.
- B. in demographic attrition because in any population a certain amount of people may decide to emigrate, or move to a different country.
- C. in demographic attrition because, in any population, a certain amount of people may decide to emigrate or move to a different country.
- D. in demographic attrition because in any population, a certain amount of people may decide to emigrate, or move to a different country.
- E. in demographic attrition because in any population a certain amount of people may decide to emigrate or move to a different country.

Item 21.
Suppose that the student was asked to write an essay, the purpose of which was to explain how the government could rectify current deficiencies in the age-sex structure. Has the student achieved this purpose?
- A. Yes, because the student talks about the government's reassessment of funding priorities.

B. Yes, because the student describes the social policy implication of the age-sex structure.
C. Yes, because the student explains the effect of governmental policy on low birth rates.
D. No, because the student fails to provide sufficient examples of the how governmental policy needs to adapt to population changes over time.
E. No, because the student does not enumerate specific solutions that the government could attempt.

ESSAY CORRECTION EXERCISE 3

[1] A group of English separatists known as the Pilgrims first left England to live in Amsterdam, in 1608. [2] After spending a few years in their new city, apart from this, many members of the group [3] felt whose they did not have enough independence. [4] Hence, in 1617, the Pilgrims decided to leave Amsterdam immigrating to America.

[5] More of these separatists were poor farmers [6] whom did not have much education or social status, and, not surprisingly, [7] the group had many financial problems that prevented them for beginning their journey. [8] Thereby their inability to finance themselves caused many disputes and disagreements, [9] the Pilgrims finally managing to obtain financing [10] from a well-known and considerable London businessman named Thomas Weston.

[11] Having secured Weston's monetary support, the group returned to England to pick up some additional passengers, [12] and it boarded a large ship called the Mayflower on September 16, 1620. [13] After 65 days at sea, the pilgrim's reached America.

[14] Plymouth a town about 35 miles southeast of Boston in the New England state of Massachusetts [15] was established by the Pilgrims in

December 21, 1620. [16] Even though the early days of this new lives were filled with hope and promise, [17] the harsh winter proved being too much for some of the settlers. [18] Near half of the Pilgrims died during that first winter, [19] but those who lived go on to work hard and prosper.

Item 1.
- A. A group of English separatists known as the Pilgrims first left England to live in Amsterdam, in 1608.
- B. A group of English separatists known as the Pilgrims first left England to live, in Amsterdam, in 1608.
- C. A group of English separatists known as the Pilgrims first left England to live in Amsterdam in 1608.
- D. A group of English separatists known as the Pilgrims, first left England to live in Amsterdam, in 1608.
- E. A group of English separatists known as the Pilgrims, first left England to live, in Amsterdam in 1608.

Item 2.
- A. After spending a few years in their new city, apart from this, many members of the group
- B. After spending a few years in their new city, in this case, many members of the group
- C. After spending a few years in their new city, namely, many members of the group
- D. After spending a few years in their new city, however, many members of the group
- E. After spending a few years in their new city, otherwise, many members of the group

Item 3.
- A. felt whose they did not have enough independence.
- B. felt whom they did not have enough independence.
- C. felt which they did not have enough independence.
- D. felt that they did not have enough independence.
- E. felt in that they did not have enough independence.

Item 4.
- A. Hence, in 1617, the Pilgrims decided to leave Amsterdam immigrating to America.
- B. Hence, in 1617, the Pilgrims decided to leave Amsterdam to immigrate to America.
- C. Hence, in 1617, the Pilgrims decided to leave Amsterdam emigrating to America.
- D. Hence, in 1617, the Pilgrims decided to leave Amsterdam to emigrate to America.
- E. Hence, in 1617, the Pilgrims decided to leave Amsterdam for migrating to America.

Item 5.
- A. More of these separatists were poor farmers
- B. Much of these separatists were poor farmers
- C. Many of these separatists were poor farmers
- D. Many more of these separatists were poor farmers
- E. The most of these separatists were poor farmers

Item 6.
- A. whom did not have much education or social status, and, not surprisingly,
- B. of whom did not have much education or social status, and, not surprisingly,
- C. whose did not have much education or social status, and, not surprisingly,
- D. which did not have much education or social status, and, not surprisingly,
- E. who did not have much education or social status, and, not surprisingly,

Item 7.
- A. the group had many financial problems that prevented them for beginning their journey.
- B. the group had many financial problems that prevented them to beginning their journey.
- C. the group had many financial problems that prevented them from beginning their journey.
- D. the group had many financial problems that prevented them against beginning their journey.

E.   the group had many financial problems that prevented them with beginning their journey.

Item 8.
   A.   Thereby their inability to finance themselves caused many disputes and disagreements,
   B.   Although their inability to finance themselves caused many disputes and disagreements,
   C.   Nevertheless their inability to finance themselves caused many disputes and disagreements,
   D.   Despite their inability to finance themselves caused many disputes and disagreements,
   E.   In spite of their inability to finance themselves caused many disputes and disagreements,

Item 9.
   A.   the Pilgrims finally managing to obtain financing
   B.   the Pilgrims finally managed obtaining financing
   C.   the Pilgrims finally were managed obtaining financing
   D.   the Pilgrims finally were managed to obtain financing
   E.   the Pilgrims finally managed to obtain financing

Item 10.
   A.   from a well-known and considerable London businessman named Thomas Weston.
   B.   From a well-known and affluent London businessman named Thomas Weston.
   C.   from a well-known and unfortunate London businessman named Thomas Weston.
   D.   from a well-known and adamant London businessman named Thomas Weston.
   E.   from a well-known and insistent London businessman named Thomas Weston.

Item 11.
   A.   Having secured Weston's monetary support, the group returned to England to pick up some additional passengers,
   B.   To have secured Weston's monetary support, the group returned to England to pick up some additional passengers,

- C. They have secured Weston's monetary support, the group returned to England to pick up some additional passengers,
- D. When they have secured Weston's monetary support, the group returned to England to pick up some additional passengers,
- E. Having secured Weston's monetary support, the group returned to England to pick up some additional passengers

Item 12.
- A. and it boarded a large ship called the Mayflower on September 16, 1620.
- B. and he or she boarded a large ship called the Mayflower on September 16, 1620.
- C. and one boarded a large ship called the Mayflower on September 16, 1620.
- D. and they boarded a large ship called the Mayflower on September 16, 1620.
- E. and those boarded a large ship called the Mayflower on September 16, 1620.

Item 13.
- A. After 65 days at sea, the pilgrim's reached America.
- B. After 65 days at sea, the Pilgrims' reached America.
- C. After 65 days at sea, the Pilgrims reached America.
- D. After 65 days at sea, Pilgrim's reached America.
- E. After 65 days at sea, Pilgrims' reached America.

Item 14.
- A. Plymouth a town about 35 miles southeast of Boston in the New England state of Massachusetts
- B. Plymouth, a town about 35 miles southeast of Boston in the New England state of Massachusetts,
- C. Plymouth, a town about 35 miles southeast of Boston in the New England, state of Massachusetts
- D. Plymouth, a town about 35 miles southeast of Boston in the New England, state of Massachusetts,
- E. Plymouth, a town about 35 miles southeast of Boston, in the New England, state of Massachusetts,

Item 15.
- A. was established by the Pilgrims in December 21, 1620.

B. was established by the Pilgrims on December 21, 1620.
C. was established by the Pilgrims at December 21, 1620.
D. was established by the Pilgrims upon December 21, 1620.
E. was established by the Pilgrims during December 21, 1620.

Item 16.
A. Even though the early days of this new lives were filled with hope and promise,
B. Even though the early days of that new lives were filled with hope and promise,
C. Even though the early days of their new lives were filled with hope and promise,
D. Even though the early days of these new live were filled with hope and promise,
E. Even though the early days of those new live were filled with hope and promise,

Item 17.
A. the harsh winter proved being too much for some of the settlers.
B. the harsh winter proved to be too much for some of the settlers.
C. the harsh winter proved to being too much for some of the settlers.
D. the harsh winter proved been too much for some of the settlers.
E. the harsh winter proved to been too much for some of the settlers.

Item 18.
A. Near half of the Pilgrims died during that first winter,
B. Nearly half of the Pilgrims died during that first winter,
C. Nearly of half of the Pilgrims died during that first winter,
D. Near of half of the Pilgrims died during that first winter,
E. Almost near half of the Pilgrims died during that first winter,

Item 19.
A. but those who lived go on to work hard and prosper.
B. but those who lived goes on to work hard and prosper.
C. but those who lived going on to work hard and prosper.
D. but those who lived went on to work hard and prosper.
E. but those who lived had went on to work hard and prosper.

Item 20.
If the student removed the last sentence of the essay, how would this affect the essay?
- A. The essay would have more emphasis on the hardships of the Pilgrims.
- B. The comments on the early days of the Pilgrims would have increased importance.
- C. The historical account of the Pilgrims would lack continuity.
- D. The essay would lack a sense of focus.
- E. The essay would lack a proper conclusion.

ESSAY CORRECTION EXERCISE 4

[1] In 1929 that electrical activity in the human brain was first discovered. [2] Hans Berger, the German psychiatrist made the discovery, [3] was despondent to find out, in contrast to, that his research was quickly dismissed by many other scientists.

[4] The work of Berger was confirmed three years later, in 1932, when Edgar Adrian a Briton, [5] clearly demonstrated that the brain, like the heart, is profuse in its electrical activity. [6] Because of Adrian's work, it know that the electrical impulses [7] in the brain called brain waves are a mixture of four different frequencies, [8] that are based on the number of electrical impulses [9] that occurring in the brain per second.

[10] Accordingly, there are four types of brain waves as follows, alpha, beta, delta, and theta. [11] Alpha waves occur in a state of relaxation, while beta waves occur when a person is alert. [12] In addition, delta waves take place for sleep, but they can also occur dysfunctionally when the brain has been severely damaged. [13] Finally, theta waves are a frequency of [14] somewhere in between alpha and delta. [15] Seems that the purpose of theta waves is solely to facilitate the combination of the other brain waves.

[16] The whole notion of brain waves feeds into the current controversy about brain death. [17] Some believe that brain death is characterized by the failure of the cerebral cortex to function. [18] On the other hand, anothers say that mere damage to the cerebral cortex is not enough. [19] They assert that brain stem function must also cease before can a person be declared dead because the cerebral cortex is responsible for other bodily processes.

Item 1.
- A. In 1929 that electrical activity in the human brain was first discovered.
- B. It in 1929 that electrical activity in the human brain was first discovered.
- C. It was in 1929 that electrical activity in the human brain was first discovered.
- D. It in 1929 was that electrical activity in the human brain was first discovered.
- E. That in 1929 electrical activity in the human brain was first discovered.

Item 2.
- A. Hans Berger, the German psychiatrist made the discovery,
- B. Hans Berger, the German psychiatrist had made the discovery,
- C. Hans Berger, the German psychiatrist who made the discovery,
- D. Hans Berger, the German psychiatrist whom made the discovery,
- E. Hans Berger, the German psychiatrist which made the discovery,

Item 3.
- A. was despondent to find out, in contrast to, that his research was quickly dismissed by many other scientists.
- B. was despondent to find out, likewise, that his research was quickly dismissed by many other scientists.
- C. was despondent to find out, but, that his research was quickly dismissed by many other scientists.

> D. was despondent to find out, though, that his research was quickly dismissed by many other scientists.
> E. was despondent to find out, although, that his research was quickly dismissed by many other scientists.

Item 4.
- A. The work of Berger was confirmed three years later, in 1932, when Edgar Adrian a Briton,
- B. The work of Berger was confirmed three years later, in 1932, when Edgar Adrian, a Briton,
- C. The work of Berger was confirmed three years later, in 1932, when Edgar Adrian a Briton
- D. The work of Berger was confirmed three years later, in 1932, when Edgar Adrian a Briton;
- E. The work of Berger was confirmed three years later, in 1932, when Edgar Adrian, a Briton;

Item 5.
- A. clearly demonstrated that the brain, like the heart, is profuse in its electrical activity.
- B. demonstrated that the clearly brain, like the heart, is profuse in its electrical activity.
- C. demonstrated that the brain, like clearly the heart, is profuse in its electrical activity.
- D. demonstrated that the brain, like the heart clearly, is profuse in its electrical activity.
- E. demonstrated that the brain, like the heart, is profuse clearly in its electrical activity.

Item 6.
- A. Because of Adrian's work, it know that the electrical impulses
- B. Because of Adrian's work, it known that the electrical impulses
- C. Because of Adrian's work, it is known that the electrical impulses
- D. Because of Adrian's work, we known that the electrical impulses
- E. Because of Adrian's work, one known that the electrical impulses

Item 7.
- A. in the brain called brain waves are a mixture of four different frequencies,
- B. in the brain, called brain waves are a mixture of four different frequencies,
- C. in the brain called brain waves, are a mixture of four different frequencies,
- D. in the brain, called brain waves, are a mixture of four different frequencies,
- E. in the brain, called brain waves, are a mixture, of four different frequencies,

Item 8.
- A. that are based on the number of electrical impulses
- B. that based on the number of electrical impulses
- C. which are based on the number of electrical impulses
- D. which based on the number of electrical impulses
- E. are based on the number of electrical impulses

Item 9.
- A. that occurring in the brain per second.
- B. that occurred in the brain per second.
- C. that had occurred in the brain per second.
- D. that have occurrence in the brain per second.
- E. that occur in the brain per second.

Item 10.
- A. Accordingly, there are four types of brain waves as follows, alpha, beta, delta, and theta.
- B. Accordingly, there are four types of brain waves as follows: alpha, beta, delta, and theta.
- C. Accordingly, there are four types of brain waves as follows; alpha, beta, delta, and theta.
- D. Accordingly, there are four types of brain waves as follows alpha, beta, delta, and theta.
- E. Accordingly, there are four types of brain waves as follows. Alpha, beta, delta, and theta.

Item 11.
- A. Alpha waves occur in a state of relaxation, while beta waves occur when a person is alert.
- B. Alpha waves occur in a state of relaxation, rather beta waves occur when a person is alert.
- C. Alpha waves occur in a state of relaxation, rather than beta waves occur when a person is alert.
- D. Alpha waves occur in a state of relaxation, instead of waves occur when a person is alert.
- E. Alpha waves occur in a state of relaxation, as for beta waves occur when a person is alert.

Item 12.
- A. In addition, delta waves take place for sleep, but they can also occur dysfunctionally when the brain has been severely damaged.
- B. In addition, delta waves take place during sleep, but they can also occur dysfunctionally when the brain has been severely damaged.
- C. In addition, delta waves take place since sleep, but they can also occur dysfunctionally when the brain has been severely damaged.
- D. In addition, delta waves take place with sleep, but they can also occur dysfunctionally when the brain has been severely damaged.
- E. In addition, delta waves take place at sleep, but they can also occur dysfunctionally when the brain has been severely damaged.

Item 13.
- A. Finally, theta waves are a frequency of
- B. Finally, theta waves are of a frequency
- C. Finally, theta waves of are a frequency
- D. Finally, of theta waves are a frequency
- E. Finally, theta waves are a of frequency

Item 14.
- A. somewhere in between alpha and delta.
- B. somewhere with between alpha and delta.
- C. somewhere in besides alpha and delta.

D. somewhere at between alpha and delta.
E. somewhere at besides alpha and delta.

Item 15.
A. Seems that the purpose of theta waves is solely to facilitate the combination of the other brain waves.
B. Seemingly that the purpose of theta waves is solely to facilitate the combination of the other brain waves.
C. It seemingly that the purpose of theta waves is solely to facilitate the combination of the other brain waves.
D. It is seemingly that the purpose of theta waves is solely to facilitate the combination of the other brain waves.
E. It seems that the purpose of theta waves is solely to facilitate the combination of the other brain waves.

Item 16.
A. The whole notion of brain waves feeds into the current controversy about brain death.
B. The whole notion of brain waves feeds at the current controversy about brain death.
C. The whole notion of brain waves feeds with the current controversy about brain death.
D. The whole notion of brain waves feeds against the current controversy about brain death.
E. The whole notion of brain waves feeds for the current controversy about brain death.

Item 17.
A. Some believe that brain death is characterized by the failure of the cerebral cortex to function.
B. Some people's belief that brain death is characterized by the failure of the cerebral cortex to function.
C. Some peoples' belief that brain death is characterized by the failure of the cerebral cortex to function.
D. Certain peoples believe that brain death is characterized by the failure of the cerebral cortex to function.
E. Certain believe that brain death is characterized by the failure of the cerebral cortex to function.

Item 18.
- A. On the other hand, anothers say that mere damage to the cerebral cortex is not enough.
- B. On the other hand, another say that mere damage to the cerebral cortex is not enough.
- C. On the other hand, others say that mere damage to the cerebral cortex is not enough.
- D. On the other hand, other say that mere damage to the cerebral cortex is not enough.
- E. On the other hand, other's say that mere damage to the cerebral cortex is not enough.

Item 19.
- A. They assert that brain stem function must also cease before can a person be declared dead because the cerebral cortex is responsible for other bodily processes.
- B. They assert that brain stem function must also cease before a person can be declared dead because the cerebral cortex is responsible for other bodily processes.
- C. They assert that brain stem function must also cease before may a person be declared dead because the cerebral cortex is responsible for other bodily processes.
- D. They assert that brain stem function must also cease before might a person can be declared dead because the cerebral cortex is responsible for other bodily processes.
- E. They assert that brain stem function must also cease before a person declared dead because the cerebral cortex is responsible for other bodily processes.

Item 20.
Imagine that the student would like to add the following sentence to the essay. What is the best location for this sentence?
Therefore, for these myriad reasons, it has become very important to measure brain activity.
- A. At the end of the first paragraph.
- B. At the end of the second paragraph.
- C. At the end of the third paragraph.
- D. At the beginning of the last paragraph.
- E. At the end of the last paragraph.

ESSAY CORRECTION EXERCISE 5

[1] Cancer, a group of mainly than 100 different types of disease, [2] occurs where cells in the body begin to divide abnormally and continue dividing and forming more cells without control or order. [3] All internal organs of the body consist of cells, which normally divide to produce more cells when the body requires them. [4] This is a natural, orderly process, that keeps human beings healthy.

[5] If a cell divides when is not necessary, a large growth called a tumor can form. [6] These tumors can usually be removed, and in many cases, they do not recurrence. [7] Unfortunately, in some cases the cancer at the original tumor spreads. [8] The spread of cancer in such way is called metastasis.

[9] There are some factors which are being known to increase the risk of cancer. [10] Smoking is the single cause largest of death from cancer in the United States. [11] One-third of the death's from cancer each year are related to smoking, [12] making tobacco use the most preventable cause of death in this country.

[13] Choice of food can also be link to cancer. [14] Research shows that there are a link between high-fat food and certain cancers, and being seriously overweight is also a cancer risk. [15] Cancer risk can be reduced with a cut down on fatty food and eating generous amounts of fruit and vegetables.

Item 1.
- A. Cancer, a group of mainly than 100 different types of disease,
- B. Cancer, a group of more than 100 different types of disease,
- C. Cancer, a group of 100 more different types of disease,
- D. Cancer, a group of mostly than 100 different types of disease,

E. Cancer, a group of almost than 100 different types of disease,

Item 2.
A. occurs where cells in the body begin to divide abnormally and continue dividing and forming more cells without control or order.
B. occurs which cells in the body begin to divide abnormally and continue dividing and forming more cells without control or order.
C. occurs in which cells in the body begin to divide abnormally and continue dividing and forming more cells without control or order.
D. occurs when cells in the body begin to divide abnormally and continue dividing and forming more cells without control or order.
E. occurs once when cells in the body begin to divide abnormally and continue dividing and forming more cells without control or order.

Item 3.
A. All internal organs of the body consist of cells, which normally divide to produce more cells when the body requires them.
B. All internal organs of the body consist of cells, which divide to normally produce more cells when the body requires them.
C. All internal organs of the body consist of cells, which divide to produce more normally cells when the body requires them.
D. All internal organs of the body consist of cells, which divide to produce more cells when normally the body requires them.
E. All internal organs of the body consist of cells, which divide to produce more cells when the body requires them normally.

Item 4.
A. This is a natural, orderly process, that keeps human beings healthy.
B. This is a natural, orderly process that keeps human beings healthy.
C. This is a natural orderly process, that keeps human beings healthy.
D. This is a natural orderly process that keeps human beings healthy.

E. This is a natural orderly, process that keeps human beings healthy.

Item 5.
A. If a cell divides when is not necessary, a large growth called a tumor can form.
B. If a cell divides when they are not necessary, a large growth called a tumor can form.
C. If a cell divides when it is not necessary, a large growth called a tumor can form.
D. If a cell divides when are not necessary, a large growth called a tumor can form.
E. If a cell divides when that not necessary, a large growth called a tumor can form.

Item 6.
A. These tumors can usually be removed, and in many cases, they do not recurrence.
B. These tumors can usually be removed, and in many cases, they do not make recurrence.
C. These tumors can usually be removed, and in many cases, they do not recurring.
D. These tumors can usually be removed, and in many cases, they do not are recurred.
E. These tumors can usually be removed, and in many cases, they do not recur.

Item 7.
A. Unfortunately, in some cases the cancer at the original tumor spreads.
B. Unfortunately, in some cases the cancer from the original tumor spreads.
C. Unfortunately, in some cases the cancer with the original tumor spreads.
D. Unfortunately, in some cases the cancer for the original tumor spreads.
E. Unfortunately, in some cases the cancer below the original tumor spreads.

Item 8.
- A. The spread of cancer in such way is called metastasis.
- B. The spread of cancer in such a way is called metastasis.
- C. The spread of cancer in such ways is called metastasis.
- D. The spread of cancer in such like way is called metastasis.
- E. The spread of cancer in such like ways is called metastasis.

Item 9.
- A. There are some factors which are being known to increase the risk of cancer.
- B. There are some factors which are know to increase the risk of cancer.
- C. There are some factors which are knowing to increase the risk of cancer.
- D. There are some factors which are known to increase the risk of cancer.
- E. There are some factors which have known to increase the risk of cancer.

Item.10
- A. Smoking is the single cause largest of death from cancer in the United States.
- B. Smoking is the single cause of largest death from cancer in the United States.
- C. Smoking is the single cause of death largest from cancer in the United States.
- D. Smoking is the single cause of death from cancer largest in the United States.
- E. Smoking is the largest single cause of death from cancer in the United States.

Item 11.
- A. One-third of the death's from cancer each year are related to smoking,
- B. One-third of the deaths' from cancer each year are related to smoking,
- C. One-third of the deaths from cancer each year are related to smoking,
- D. One-third of cancer's deaths each year are related to smoking,
- E. One-third of cancers' deaths each year are related to smoking,

Item 12.
- A. making tobacco use the most preventable cause of death in this country.
- B. which making tobacco use the most preventable cause of death in this country.
- C. made tobacco use the most preventable cause of death in this country.
- D. which will be making tobacco use the most preventable cause of death in this country.
- E. in making tobacco use the most preventable cause of death in this country.

Item 13.
- A. Choice of food can also be link to cancer.
- B. Choice of food can also be linking to cancer.
- C. Choice of food can also be linked to cancer.
- D. Choice of food can also been linked to cancer.
- E. Choice of food can also link to cancer.

Item 14.
- A. Research shows that there are a link between high-fat food and certain cancers, and being seriously overweight is also a cancer risk.
- B. Research shows that there is a link between high-fat food and certain cancers, and being seriously overweight is also a cancer risk.
- C. Research shows that there's links between high-fat food and certain cancers, and being seriously overweight is also a cancer risk.
- D. Research shows that there is existing a link between high-fat food and certain cancers, and being seriously overweight is also a cancer risk.
- E. Research shows that there in existence a link between high-fat food and certain cancers, and being seriously overweight is also a cancer risk.

Item 15.
- A. Cancer risk can be reduced with a cut down on fatty food and eating generous amounts of fruit and vegetables.
- B. Cancer risk can be reduced with cutting down on fatty food and eating generous amounts of fruit and vegetables.
- C. Cancer risk can be reduced with cutting down fatty food and eating generous amounts of fruit and vegetables.
- D. Cancer risk can be reduced by cutting down on fatty food and eating generous amounts of fruit and vegetables.
- E. Cancer risk can be reduced by cut down on fatty food and eating generous amounts of fruit and vegetables.

Item 16.
Suppose the student wants to include an admonition to the reader about how he or she can prevent cancer risks. Which sentence, if added to the end of the essay, would achieve this purpose?
- A. Accordingly, the government needs to act now to help improve the health of the country.
- B. Militating against the causes of cancer is a difficult but necessary task.
- C. It is therefore the responsibility of each individual to try to mitigate cancer risk by living a healthy lifestyle.
- D. However, these deaths could easily have been avoided.
- E. Nevertheless, most people agree that trying to prevent cancer risk is extremely important.

ASWERS TO THE ESSAY CORRECTION EXERCISES

Antarctica Essay

1. A
2. C
3. D
4. C
5. A
6. B
7. B
8. B
9. D
10. C
11. A
12. B
13. C
14. B
15. B
16. E
17. C
18. B
19. D
20. E

Population Age-Sex Structure Essay

1. D
2. B
3. A
4. E
5. B
6. C
7. D
8. B
9. C
10. B
11. C
12. B
13. D
14. C
15. E
16. D
17. C
18. B
19. A
20. D
21. E

The Pilgrims Essay

1. C
2. D
3. D
4. D
5. C
6. E
7. C
8. B
9. E
10. B
11. A
12. D
13. C
14. B
15. B
16. C
17. B
18. B
19. D
20. E

Brain Wave Research Essay

1. C
2. C
3. D
4. B
5. A
6. C
7. D
8. C
9. E
10. B
11. A
12. B
13. B
14. A
15. E
16. A
17. A
18. C
19. B
20. E

Cancer Risk Essay

1. B
2. D
3. A
4. B
5. C
6. E
7. B
8. B
9. D
10. E
11. C
12. A
13. C
14. B
15. D
16. C

www.ingramcontent.com/pod-product-compliance
Lightning Source LLC
Chambersburg PA
CBHW082028120526
44592CB00038B/2284